Sketch Page

Homemade Mistakes

Topher Kearby

2019

Contact me at:

www.topherkearby.com

@topherkearby

Instagram, Twitter, and Facebook

TopherKearby@gmail.com

Homemade Mistakes

Cover Design by Jeremiah Lambert

www.jeremiahlambertart.com

www.TopherKearby.com

ISBN: 13: 978-0-578-46756-6

Edited by Topher Kearby and Christina Hart

Trade Paperback Edition

Printed in the United States of America

Gray Force Publishing

Part One:

Handmade words.

No edits. No chance to make things perfect. I typed and sketched these pieces all over America. Feel free to rip out your favorite pieces and give them away or paper your wall.

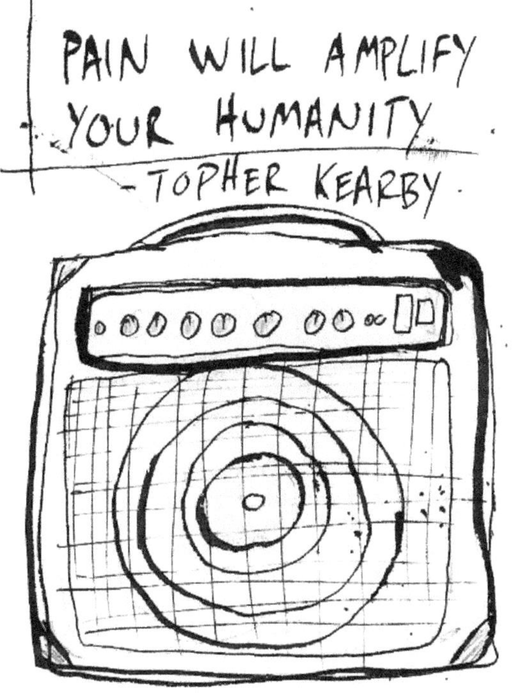
PAIN WILL AMPLIFY
YOUR HUMANITY
-TOPHER KEARBY

ALONE

to be alone
with yourself is one thing.
maybe it's good or maybe
it's a bit lonely,
but it's okay in the end.

to be alone
with another person is
something quite different.
it's cold like winter.
it's painful like frostbite.
it's an ~~emptiness~~ emptiness
like no other because you
are with another that will
never understand who you
really are.

- topher kearby

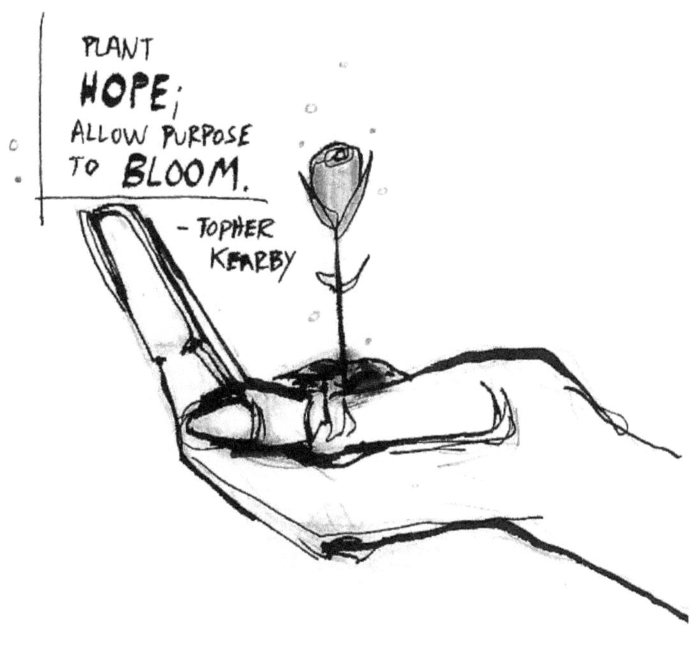
PLANT
HOPE;
ALLOW PURPOSE
TO BLOOM.
- TOPHER
KEARBY

BELIEVE

people will look at
you with crooked
questioning smiles
when you tell them
you are quitting it
all to go after your
dreams.
they will pile doubt
on your shoulders.
they will roll their
eyes at your plans.
they will try to stop
you from moving
forward.

but it isn't because
they don't believe in
you,
it's because they don't
believe in themselves.

- topher kearby

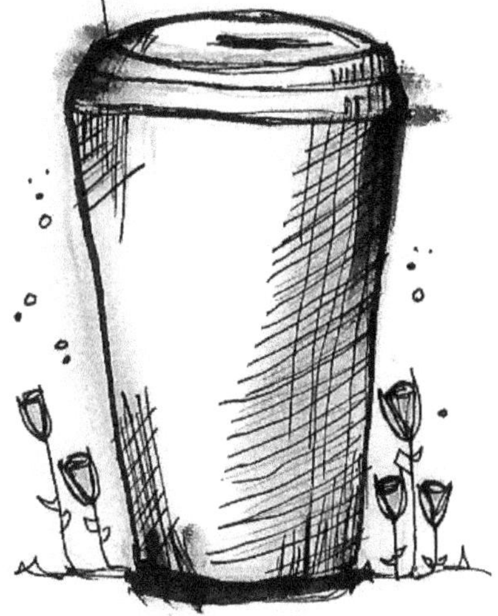
hot coffee and
WILD HOPE,
some mornings
that is enough.
- topher kearby

i read a story once about
a bridge on the edge of
nowhere. it lead somewhere
but no one was quite sure
to where exactly. you see,
everyone was afraid to walk
across its wooden planks to
the other side, so no one
ever did. until one day when
a stranger came to town,
that's how these stories go.
yes, she came to town and
walked right across that
bridge to somewhere as if it
were no big thing at all,
and i guess it wasn't because
she came back a few days
later and couldn't have
seemed happier. everyone
asked her, "so where did
the bridge take you?"
she replied, "exactly where
i needed to be. somewhere
new."
and that made everyone who
never crossed over feel a
bit sad they were never brave
enough to see where the bridge
went, but they should't feel
too badly. sometimes it takes
someone who doesn't know she
should be afraid to remind
everyone else that there isn't
really anything to fear
in the first place.

- topher kearby

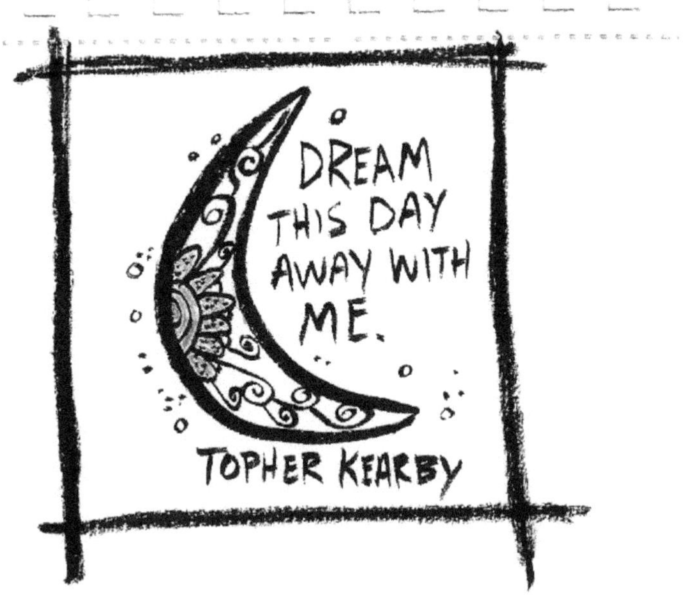
DREAM
THIS DAY
AWAY WITH
ME.
TOPHER KEARBY

CAREFUL

be cautious opening your
heart to someone new.
be careful.
at first.
and careful still after
some time has passed.
make sure that this new
person is really true.
truly real.
test the relationship out
for a while - lover or
family or friend.
take time.
because once your heart
is open it can be helped
or harmed,
and life is too short
spending all of your time
repairing damage done by
someone who never intended
to take care of your heart.

careful.

- topher kearby

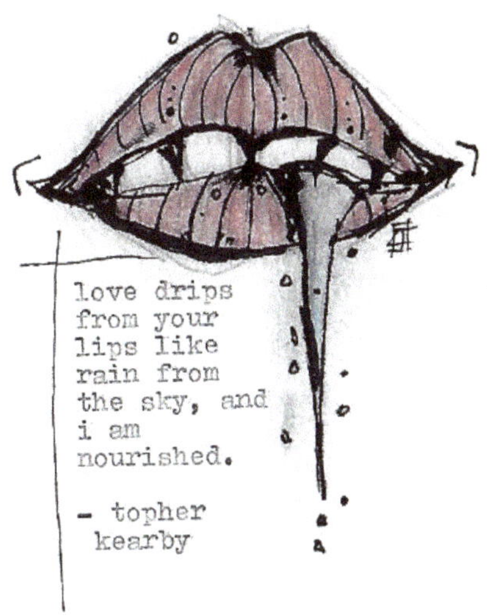
love drips
from your
lips like
rain from
the sky, and
i am
nourished.
- topher
kearby

CHILDREN

tell your children to not
grow up.
don't tell them to not grow
up too fast, no.
tell them to not grow up at
all. ever.
growing up steals imagination
and wonder like greedy thief.
a
never grow up.
never surrender the hope that
lives inside a youthful spirit,
for the world needs more dreamers
and wonderers and bright minds
full of WHAT COULD BE.
and less black leather briefcases
filled with regret.

- topher kearby

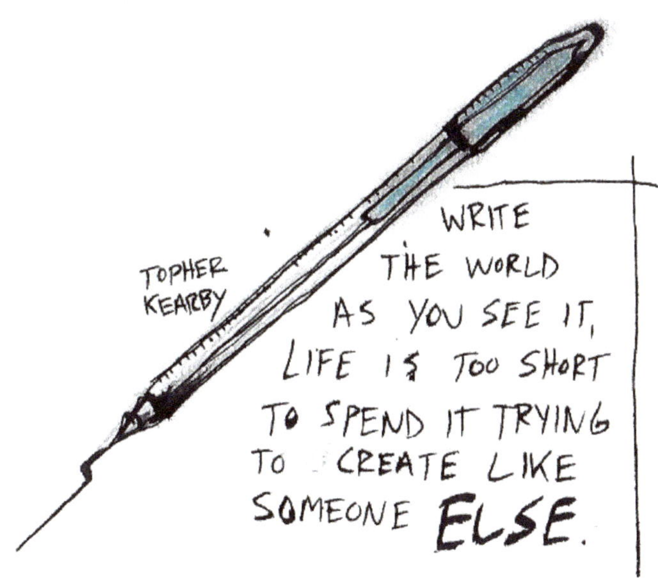
TOPHER KEARBY
WRITE
THE WORLD
AS YOU SEE IT,
LIFE IS TOO SHORT
TO SPEND IT TRYING
TO CREATE LIKE
SOMEONE ELSE.

COFFEE

when i wake up á stumble
across my bedroom floor
and find my way to the
kitchen. there is a wíndow
over my sink and on sunny
days the light hurts my
eyes in the best of ways.
i grab a mug. i start the
coffee machine. and i wait
for the distinctive aroma
to fill the room. i grab
my mug once again, this
time it's filled with the
good stuff, and i open my
front pxxxk door and sit
out on my porch and drink
my coffee.
and i am happy.

- topher kearby

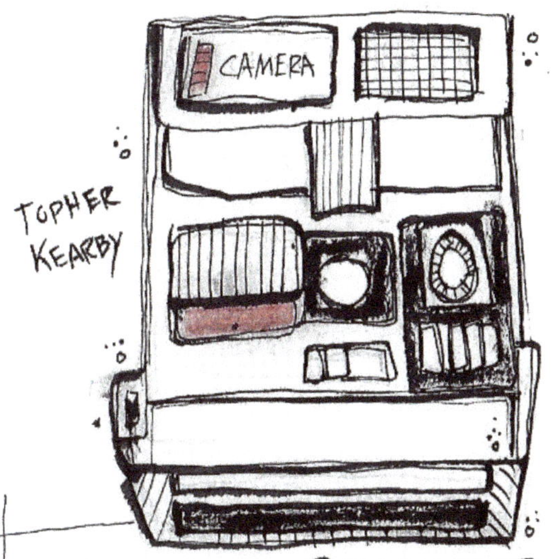

I WANT TO REMEMBER THIS MOMENT FOREVER, LIKE A PHOTOGRAGH THAT NEVER FADES.

FATHER

as a father i just want my
girls to be happy and whole.
i know what life is
and i know that it can be cold.
so i worry.
and i plan.
i try to be an example of what
a good person is, but it's
complicated.
life is complicated.

but love is simple and that is
what i focus on.
we all make mistakes.
we all have bad days and good
days and we fall and we stand
once again.

that's okay.
that's called being human
and i hope i show them
that being human is the best
way to live.

if you're reading this, girls,
please know that i love you
and always will.
and if you're not reading this
then you and Stephen King have
something in common.

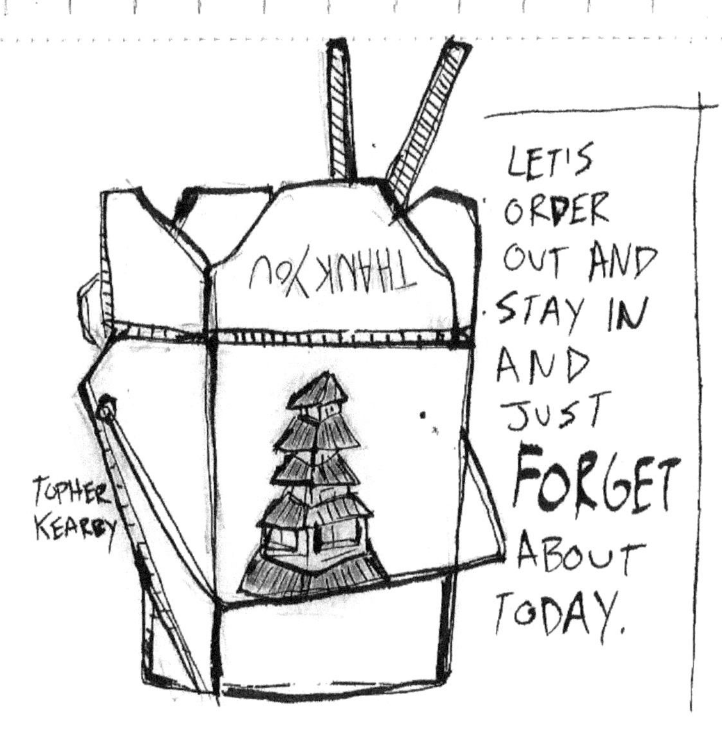
THANK YOU
TOPHER
KEARBY
LET'S
ORDER
OUT AND
STAY IN
AND
JUST
FORGET
ABOUT
TODAY.

HAPPINESS

happiness is a gift
they say,
those ones that say
all the simple words
at the ones asking for
complex answers.
but it isn't.
happiness is a choice,
a desire, a pursuit,
and a lifelong goal.
it doesn't happen as
if it were rain in May,
it is earned.
over and over again every
day until there are no
more days.
and maybe that is the
secret to life -
to not give up on
happiness because there
is still time left to
discover it for yourself.

so go do that.
find what makes your heart
soar and go after it with
everything you've got.

- topher kearby

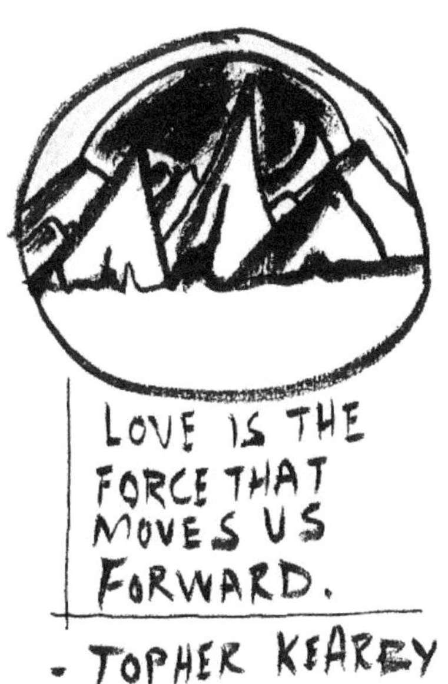
LOVE IS THE
FORCE THAT
MOVES US
FORWARD.
- TOPHER KEARBY

i am told that there is an
invisible eye that rests in
the center of my mind.
it sees beyond the here and
now, staring intensely into
the wxtx what could be, or
perhaps into the what already
is but can't be seen with any
other eyes. i feel every now
and thamxixxtxpx then that i
see with that third eye and
everything is so clear for
a moment. the world slows.
words have new meaning. time
freezes and i am at peace.
not a nice peace or a kind peace
but a total and consuming peace.
and it is wonderful.

- topher kearby

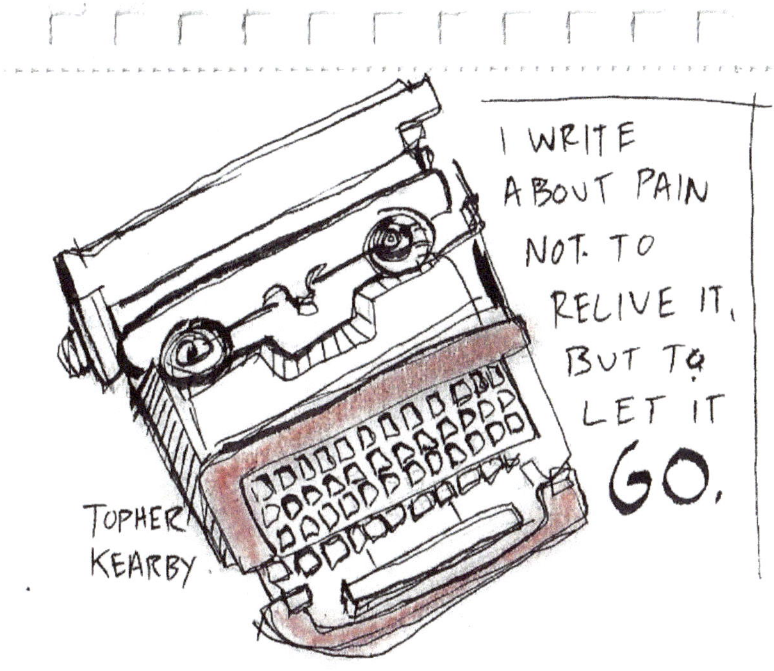

I WRITE
ABOUT PAIN
NOT TO
RELIVE IT,
BUT TO
LET IT
GO.

TOPHER
KEARBY

KISS

sure.
there isn't a right way
to kiss someone,
but there is a wong way
and there is a better way.

the wrong way is to kiss
wanting to only be kissed
back. it's a selfish kind
of thing that will leave
a rotten taste in your
mouth.

the better way to kiss
is after a long conversation
about everything and nothing.
it doesn't have to be long
and you don't need to feel
like it's important,
but i promise you that
kiss will be remembered.

- topher kearby

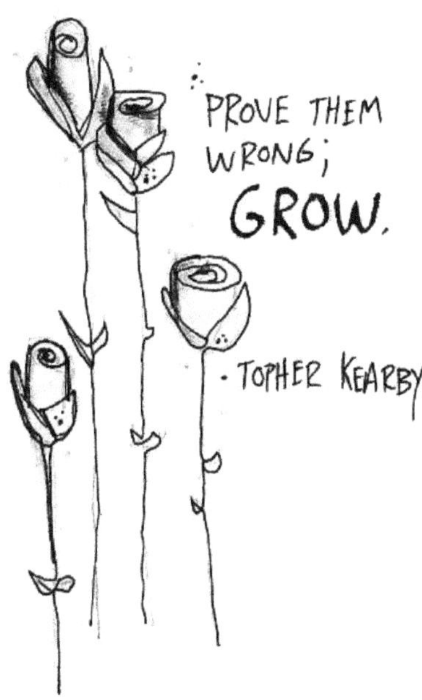
PROVE THEM
WRONG;
GROW.
- TOPHER KEARBY

MAGIC

i open the window and
the wind moves past me
as if it were looking
for me at this moment.
it can't be true but
then again this world
is filled with magic
that still can't be
fully explained. i like
that. the idea that
there is still so much
that is unknown. less
now than there once
was, sure, but still
just look up at the
stars and it becomes
easy to realize how
little we truly understand,
a wise man might say,
"no. no. there is no
magic. what we do not
know we will learn."
but the dreamer will say,
"yes, exactly. the magic
is in the discovery."

- topher kearby

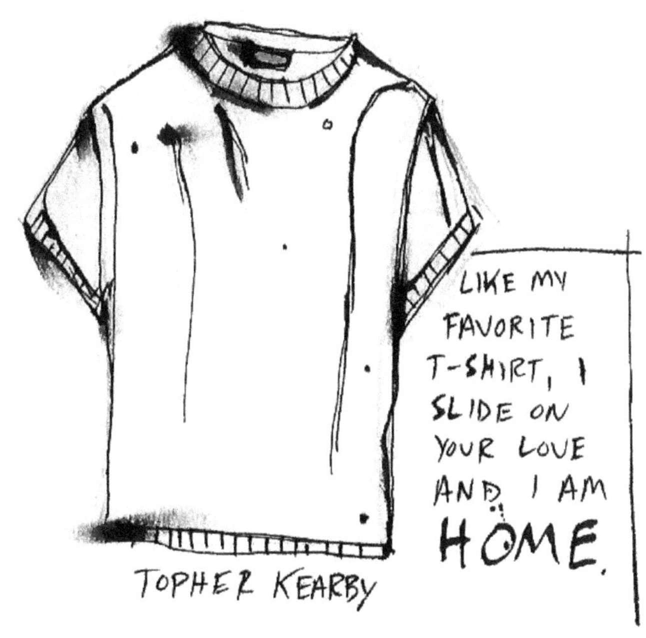
LIKE MY
FAVORITE
T-SHIRT, I
SLIDE ON
YOUR LOVE
AND I AM
HOME.
TOPHER KEARBY

MORE

there are moments in life
that require more.
more time.
more hope.
more love.
more strength.
more of you.
don't dare be afraid of
those times.
don't dare worry that
who you are will not
be enough,
because you are more
than enough.
you are more than ready
for what's next.

- topher kearby

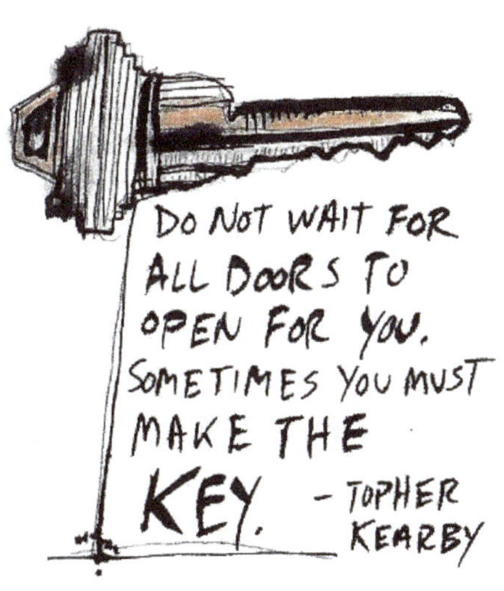
DO NOT WAIT FOR
ALL DOORS TO
OPEN FOR YOU.
SOMETIMES YOU MUST
MAKE THE
KEY.
- TOPHER
KEARBY

we are told that perfection
is a pursuit,
and that it is a goal that
can be achieved.
so, we go about the business
of becoming perfect people.
we buy products, take classes,
work incredibly hard, and
give ourselves over to this
idea that we can be, no -
that we should be perfect;
this lifestyle is destructive.

perfection is not a pursuit,
it is a commodity sold to
each of us by people who hope
we never realize how perfect
we already are with our
glorious imperfections.

- topher kearby

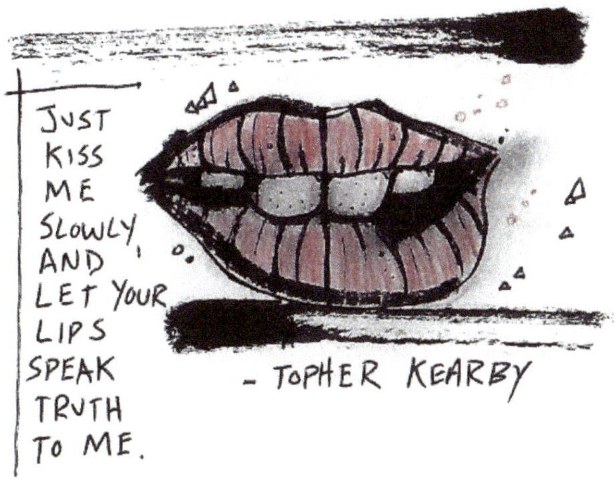
JUST
KISS
ME
SLOWLY,
AND
LET YOUR
LIPS
SPEAK
TRUTH
TO ME.
- TOPHER KEARBY

PROMISED

nothing is promised in this
life and if you think so then
i feel sorry for you.
don't wake up expecting to
be given what you want,
instead wake up and make
a plan to earn what you
want. it's not a secret
or a mystery.

if you want to be anything
or do anything worth
anything,
you need to put in the work.

- topher kearby

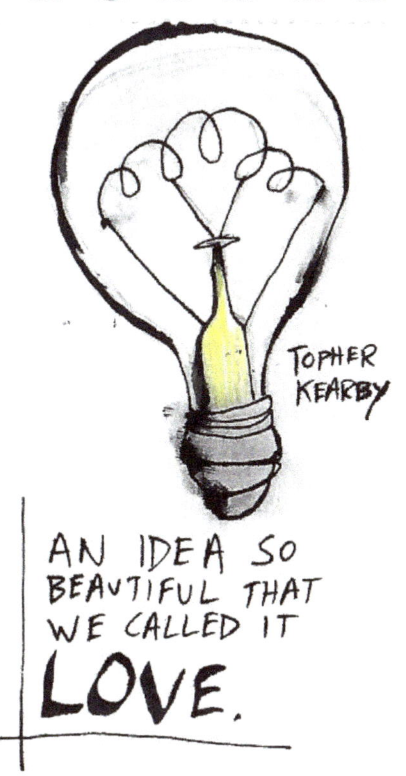
TOPHER
KEARBY
AN IDEA SO
BEAUTIFUL THAT
WE CALLED IT
LOVE.

RAIN

give them their money
and power and fame.

i'll take your hand in
mine while the two of
us take a long walk
in the rain.

- topher kearby

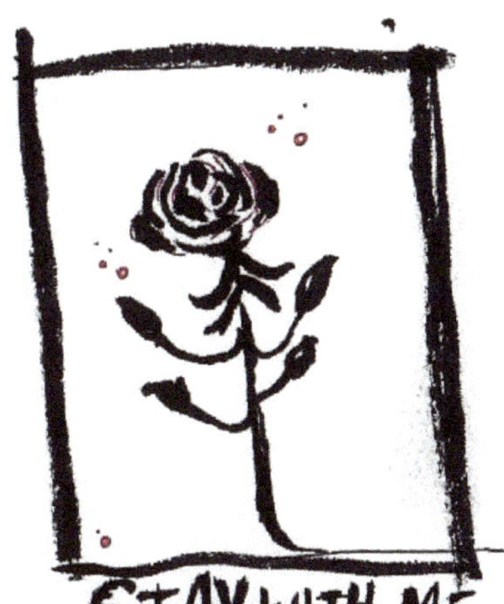

STAY WITH ME
GROW WITH ME
LOVE WITH ME
- TOPHER KEARBY

SOUL

if you rip away my skin
and flesh,
dig down deep way past
my bones,
you'll see a pulsing
beating heart and a
stunning, shining soul.

- topher kearby

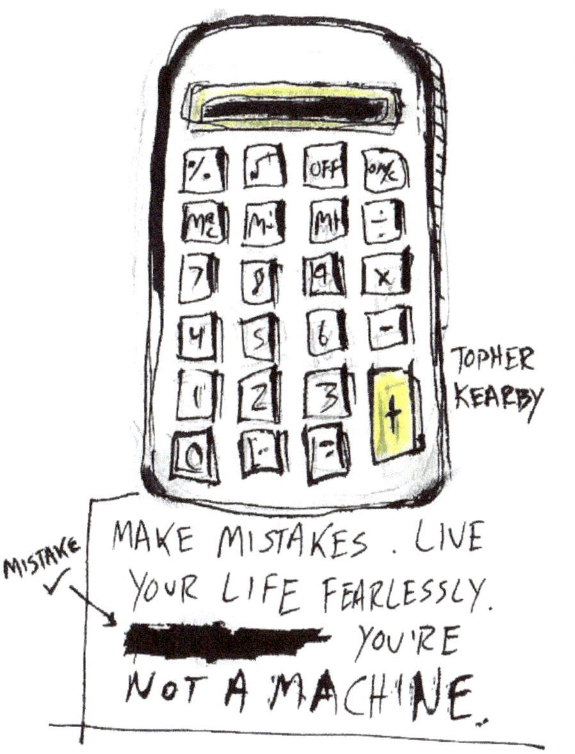
TOPHER KEARBY
MISTAKE
MAKE MISTAKES. LIVE YOUR LIFE FEARLESSLY.
YOU'RE NOT A MACHINE.

STREAM

there is a small creek
just behind my little
house and it's quite beautiful
to watch during a rain.
the dry rocks that line the
creek bank become slick with
vibrant colors.
gray becomes blue and rust
becomes crimson.
and the noise of the water
rushing past the fallen
branches that are scattered
throughout the winding
creekbed is mesmerizing.
it isn't deep enough to
be considered a stream, but
in my mind this creek is
a mighty river.
and it carries me home.

- topher kearby

FIND THE ONE WHO
HEARS YOUR MUSIC
THE SAME
WAY YOU DO.

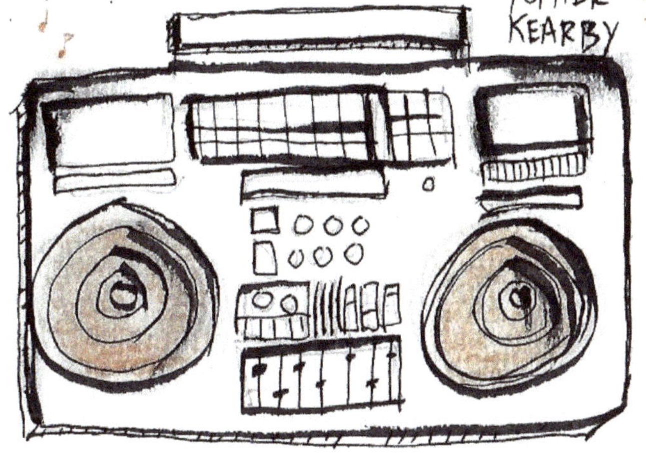

THIS

this is life.
this moving and bending
into something new each
and every day.
this is love.
this learning and growing
and becoming something
beautiful.
this is us.
this unlikely pairing
of two souls that never
knew they needed one
another so perfectly.
this is now.
this is forever.
this is good.

- topher kearby

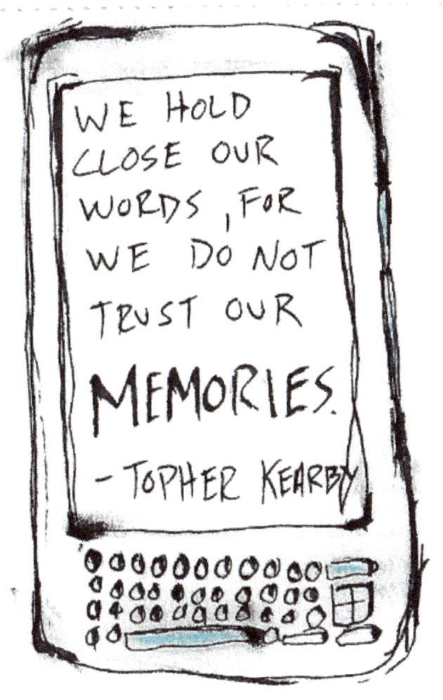
WE HOLD
CLOSE OUR
WORDS, FOR
WE DO NOT
TRUST OUR
MEMORIES.
-TOPHER KEARBY

WEIRD

this has been a weird
day.
i can't say why exactly
it has been weird,
but it has...been weird.
maybe it was the man at
the donut shop who just
ordered white milk, or
the fox that stood in
my driveway for half an
hour seemingly expecting
me to invite him inside.
weird.
strange.
as if the world tilted
a little more to one
side this morning and
everything and everyone
stood a bit crooked for
a while.

i'd be lying if i said
i didn't love it.

- topher kearby

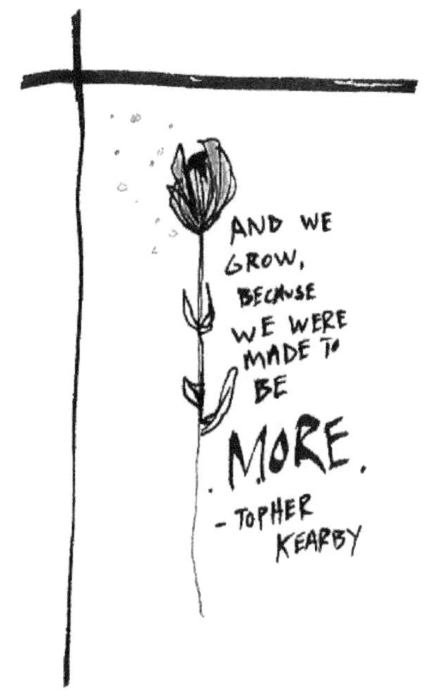
AND WE
GROW,
BECAUSE
WE WERE
MADE TO
BE
MORE.
- TOPHER
KEARBY

WORLD

take your phone and just
go outside and start
walking. somewhere. anywhere.
just get going. right now.

on your walk just look around
and soak in everything that
is around you. snap a picture.
shoot a videox. make a memory.

life is too short to waste
not getting out and seeing
what you never have truly
seen before.

- topher kearby

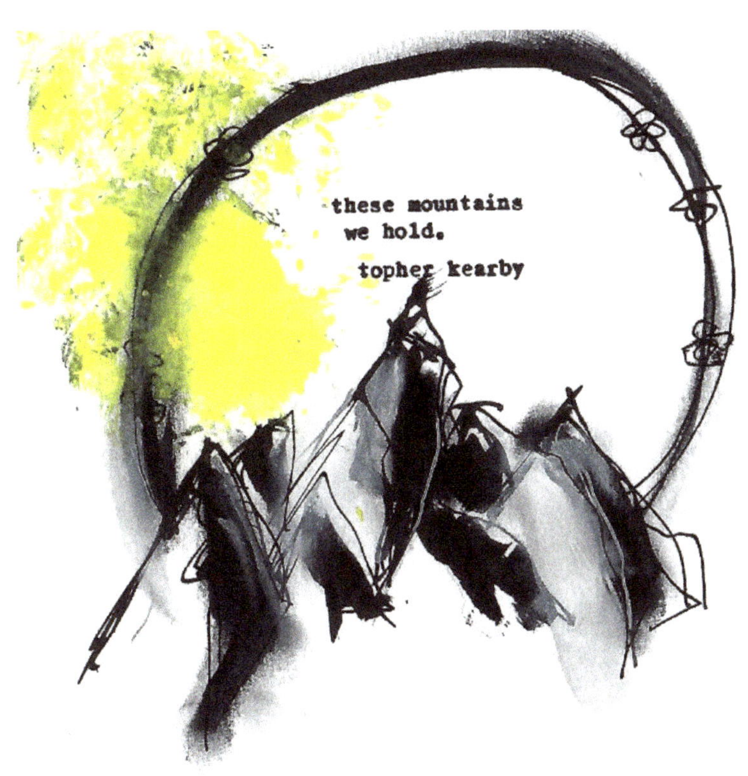
these mountains
we hold.
topher kearby

some days it feels as if i'm
faking this "human thing."
i am flesh and blood.
i am hopes and fears.
but i am also nothing some
days - nothing feels real.

mayxbexthxx maybe that's how
we all are at some points in
our lives. the world has given
too much or we have given it
too much, so we are left with
all of it or none of it and
that makes everything feel
strange...
i feel strange sometimes;
that's the best way to put it.
i am a fish in the sky or a
bird in the lake,
but either way
i can't breathe.

- topher kearby

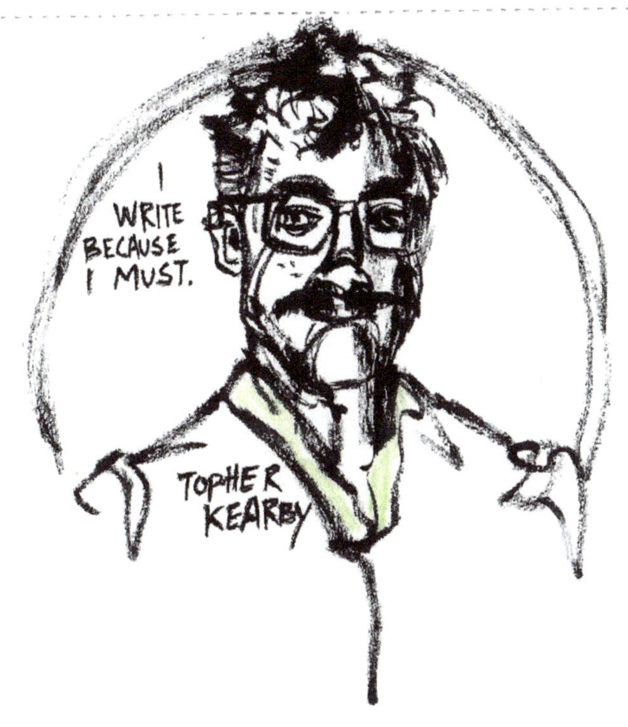
I WRITE BECAUSE I MUST.
TOPHER KEARBY

LATE NIGHTS
ARE FOR FAST FOOD
AND SLOW MOMENTS
SPENT WITH FRIENDS.

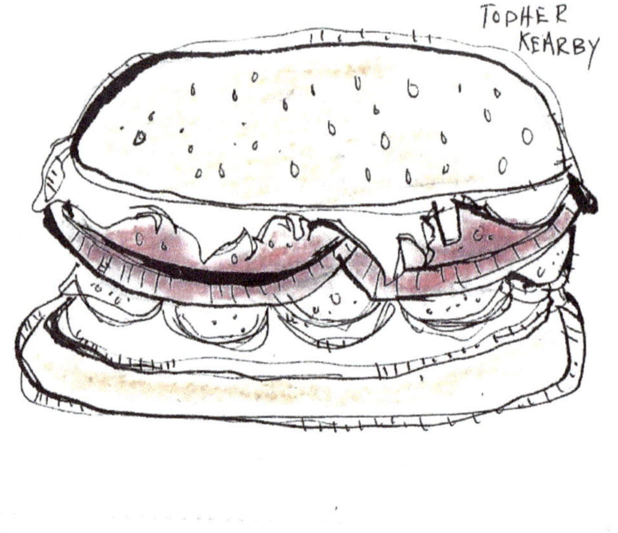

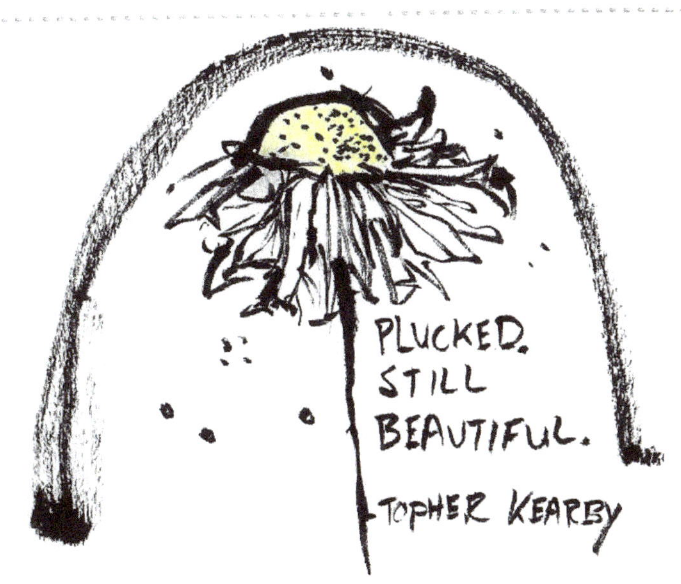
PLUCKED.
STILL
BEAUTIFUL.
-TOPHER KEARBY

PAINT
YOUR
TRUTH
AS
LOUDLY
AS YOU
CAN.

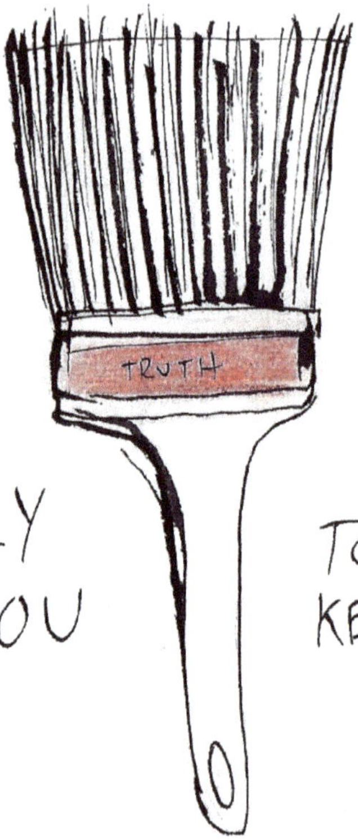

TRUTH

TOPHER
KEARBY

A GOOD MEAL &

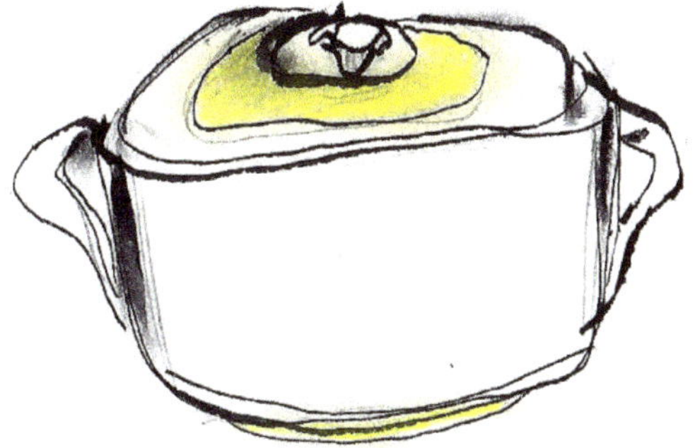

A GOOD CONVERSATION IS HAPPINESS. [TOPHER KEARBY]

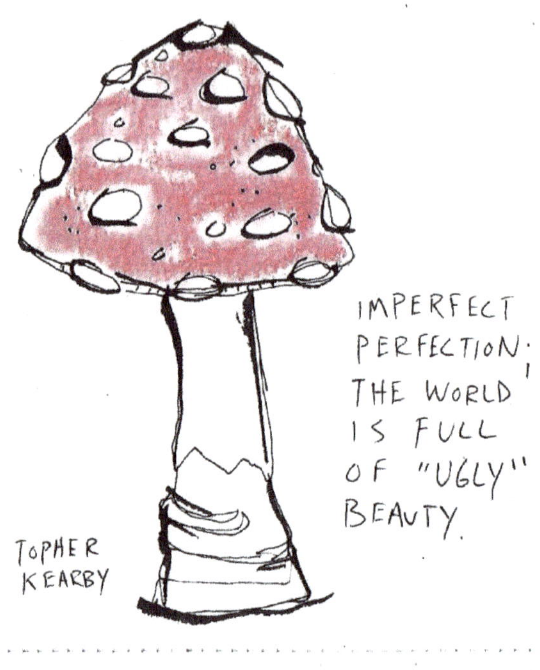
IMPERFECT PERFECTION; THE WORLD IS FULL OF "UGLY" BEAUTY.
TOPHER KEARBY

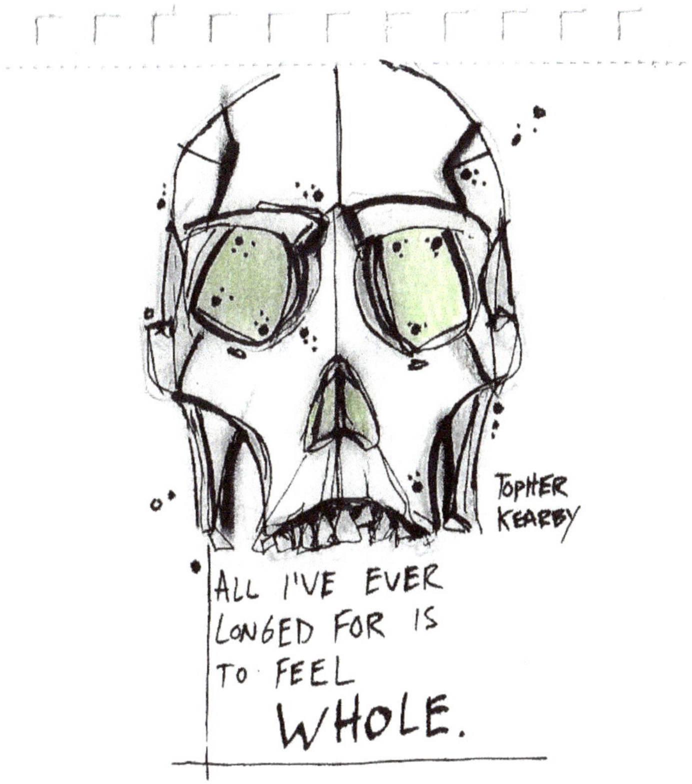

TOPHER KEARBY

ALL I'VE EVER
LONGED FOR IS
TO FEEL
WHOLE.

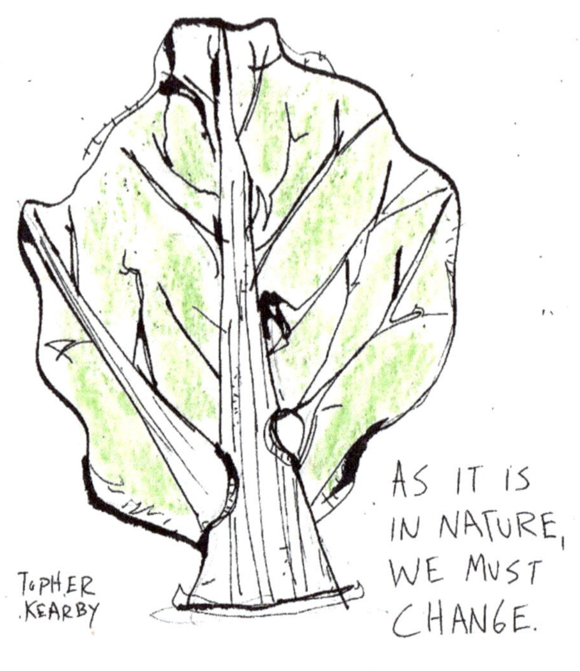
AS IT IS
IN NATURE,
WE MUST
CHANGE.
TOPHER
KEARBY

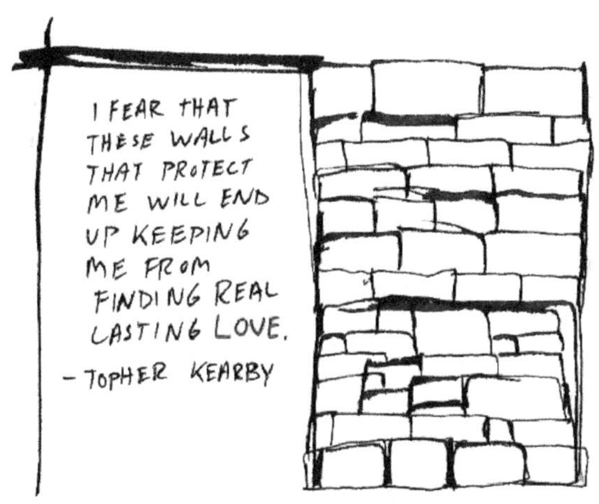
I FEAR THAT
THESE WALLS
THAT PROTECT
ME WILL END
UP KEEPING
ME FROM
FINDING REAL
LASTING LOVE.
- TOPHER KEARBY

WHAT ONCE WAS
STILL IS,
JUST IN A WAY
IT WASN'T
BEFORE.

- TOPHER KEARBY

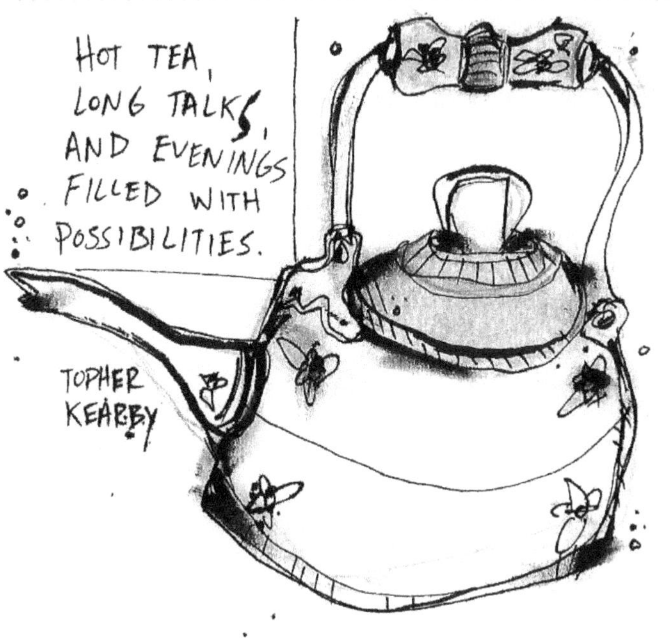
HOT TEA,
LONG TALKS,
AND EVENINGS
FILLED WITH
POSSIBILITIES.
TOPHER
KEARBY

KEEP MOVING,
KEEP FIGHTING,
YOUR BEST
DAYS ARE
STILL TO
COME.

- TOPHER
KEARBY

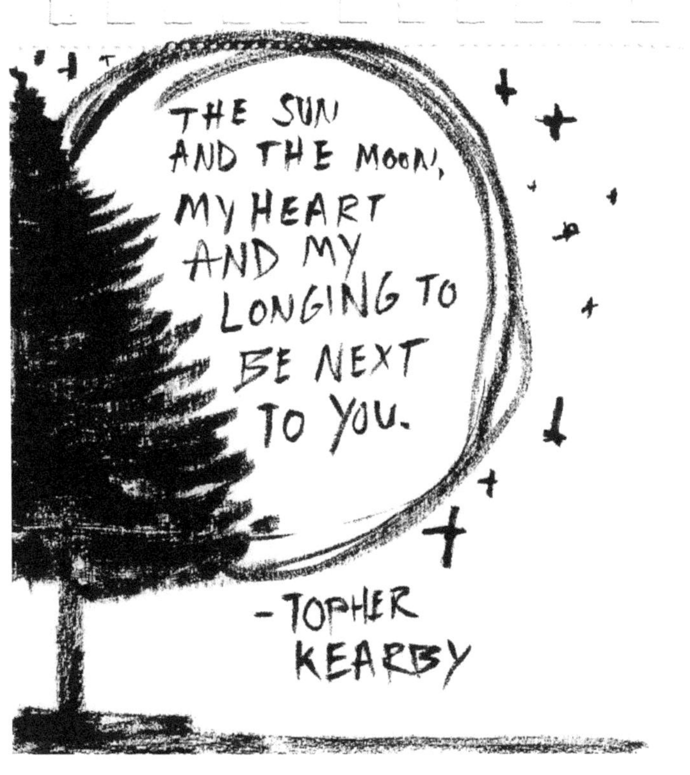
THE SUN
AND THE MOON,
MY HEART
AND MY
LONGING TO
BE NEXT
TO YOU.
-TOPHER
KEARBY

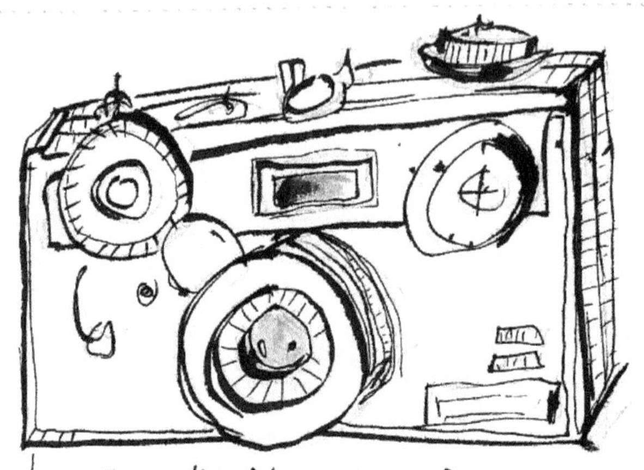
IF ONLY YOU COULD
SEE YOURSELF AS I
SEE YOU, THEN YOU WOULD
NEVER DOUBT YOUR
STRENGTH.
- TOPHER KEARBY

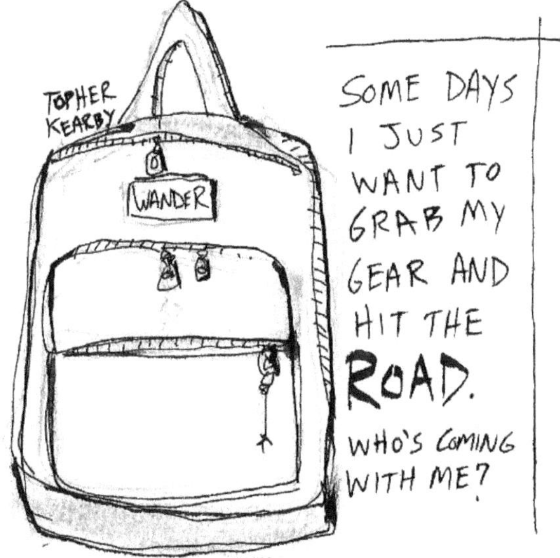
TOPHER KEARBY
WANDER
SOME DAYS I JUST WANT TO GRAB MY GEAR AND HIT THE ROAD.
WHO'S COMING WITH ME?

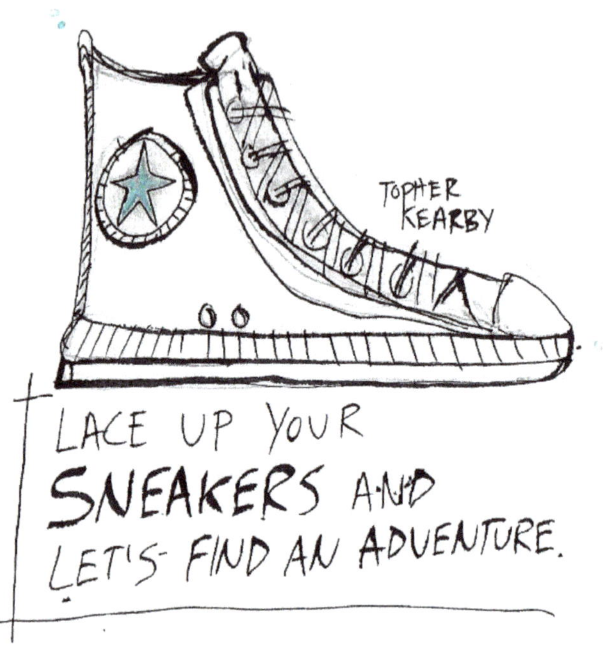
TOPHER
KEARBY
LACE UP YOUR
SNEAKERS AND
LET'S FIND AN ADVENTURE.

Part Two:

Handmade art.

A collection of original art that I've made over the past couple of years. Watercolors, inks, colored pencils, acrylics, and whatever else I could get my hands on. Check out www.topherkearby.com for all sorts of interesting art.

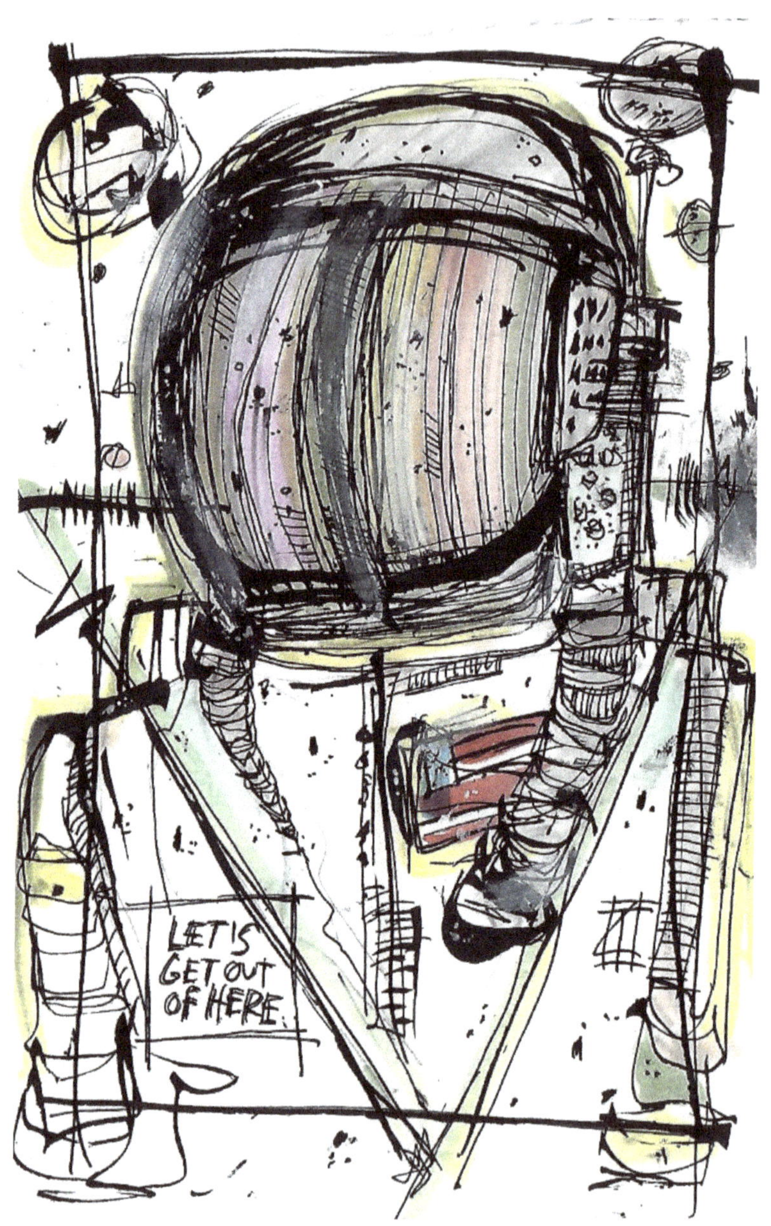
LET'S
GET OUT
OF HERE

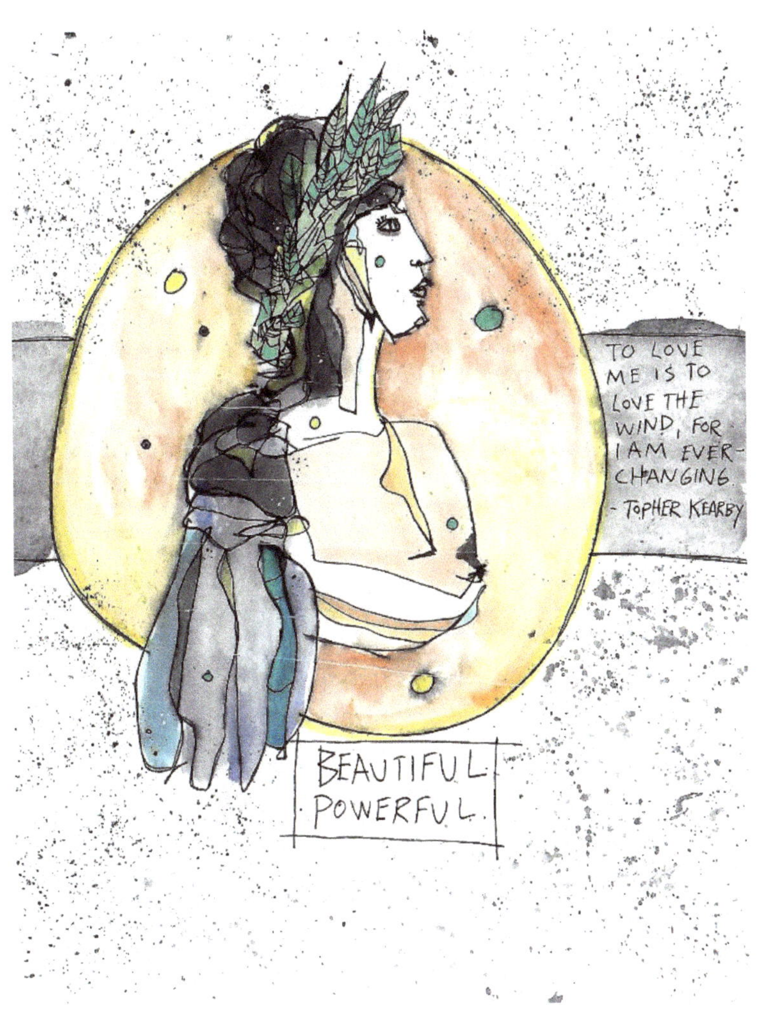
TO LOVE ME IS TO LOVE THE WIND, FOR I AM EVER-CHANGING.
- TOPHER KEARBY
BEAUTIFUL.
POWERFUL.

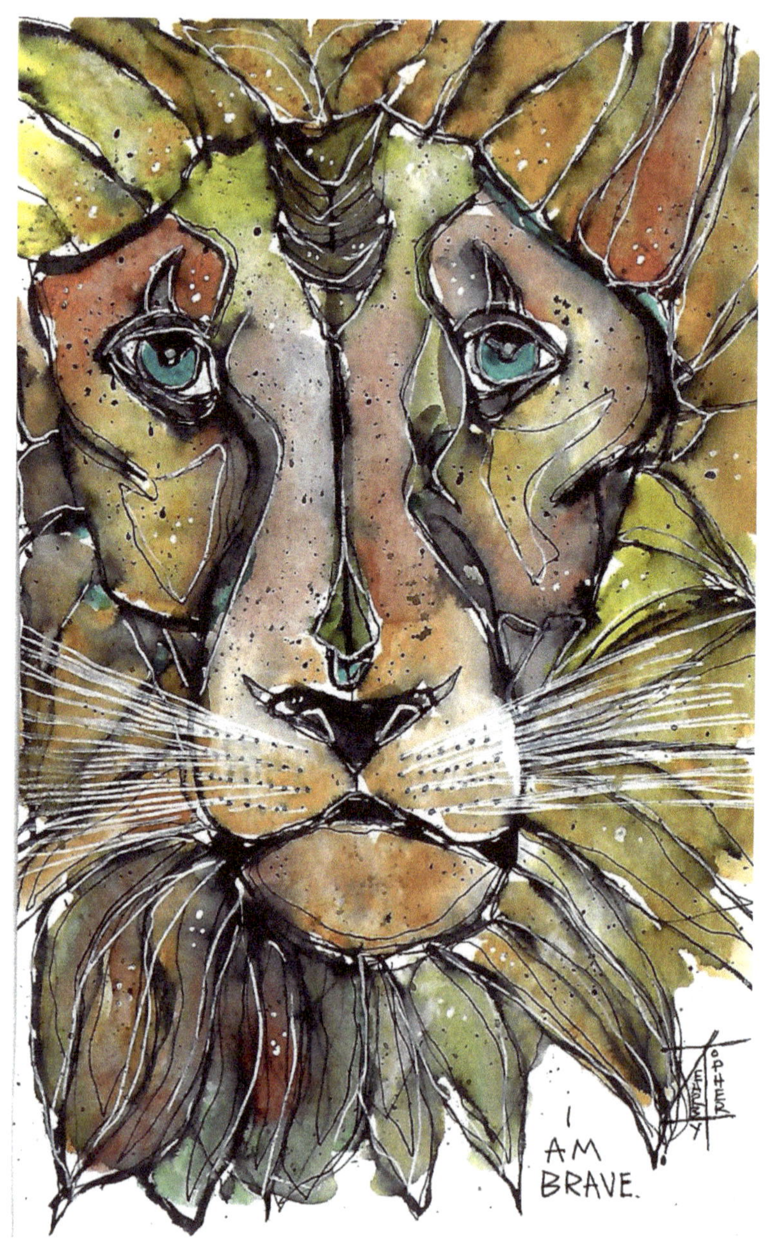
I
AM
BRAVE.

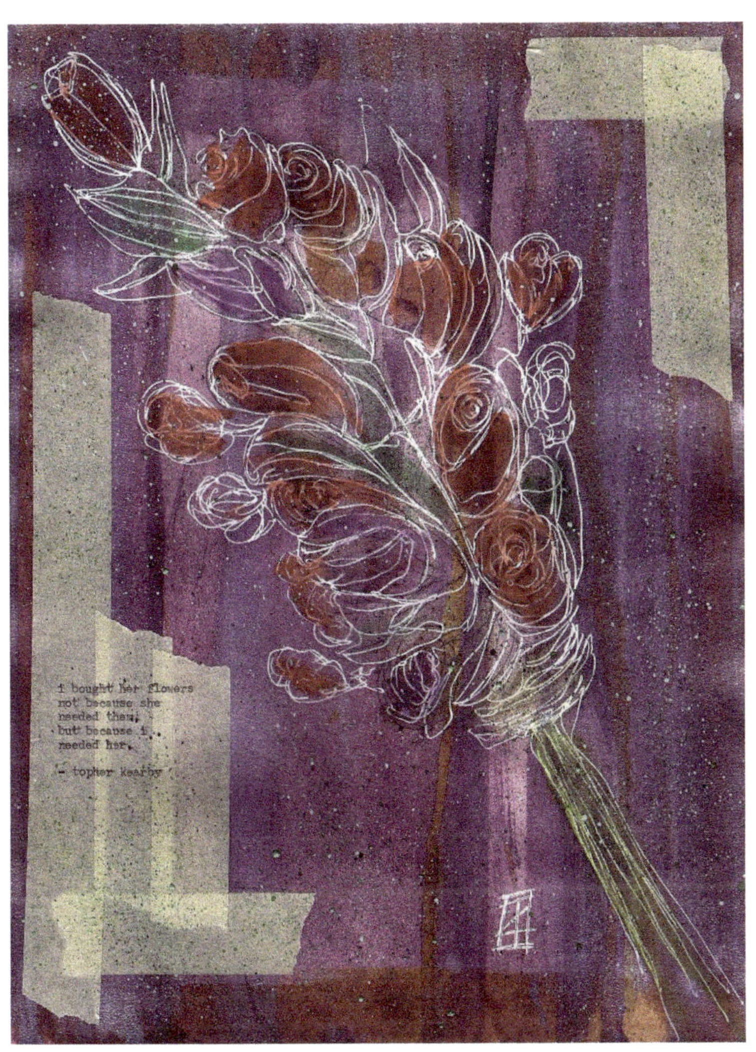
i bought her flowers
not because she
needed them,
but because i
needed her.
- topher kearby

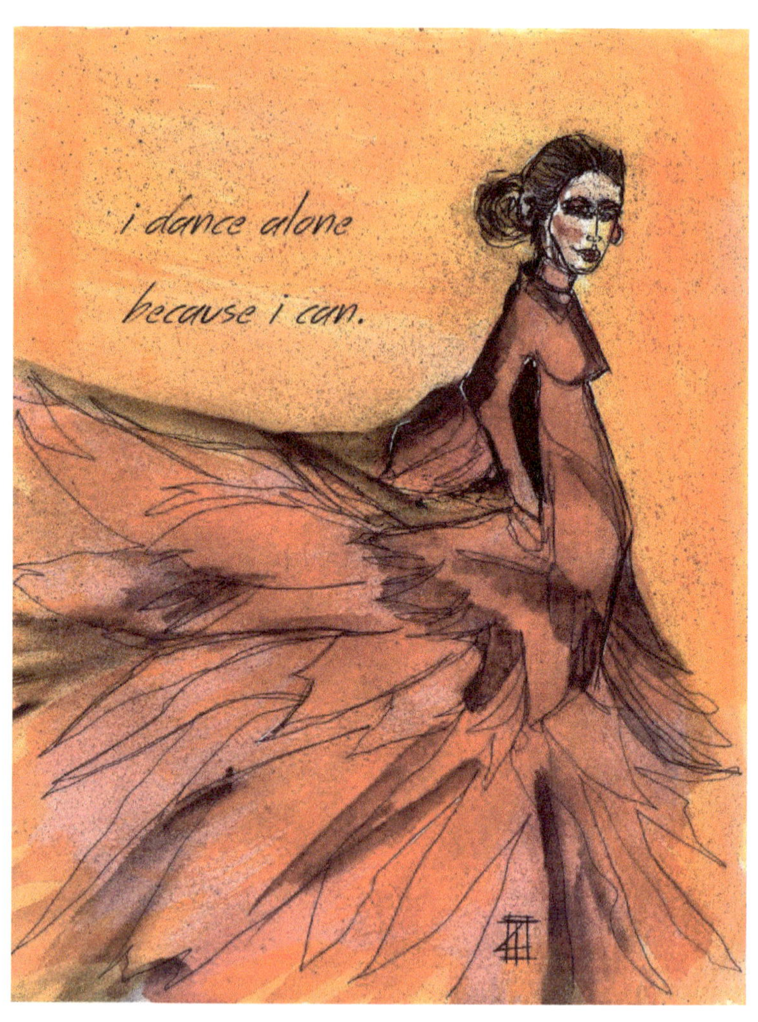
i dance alone
because i can.

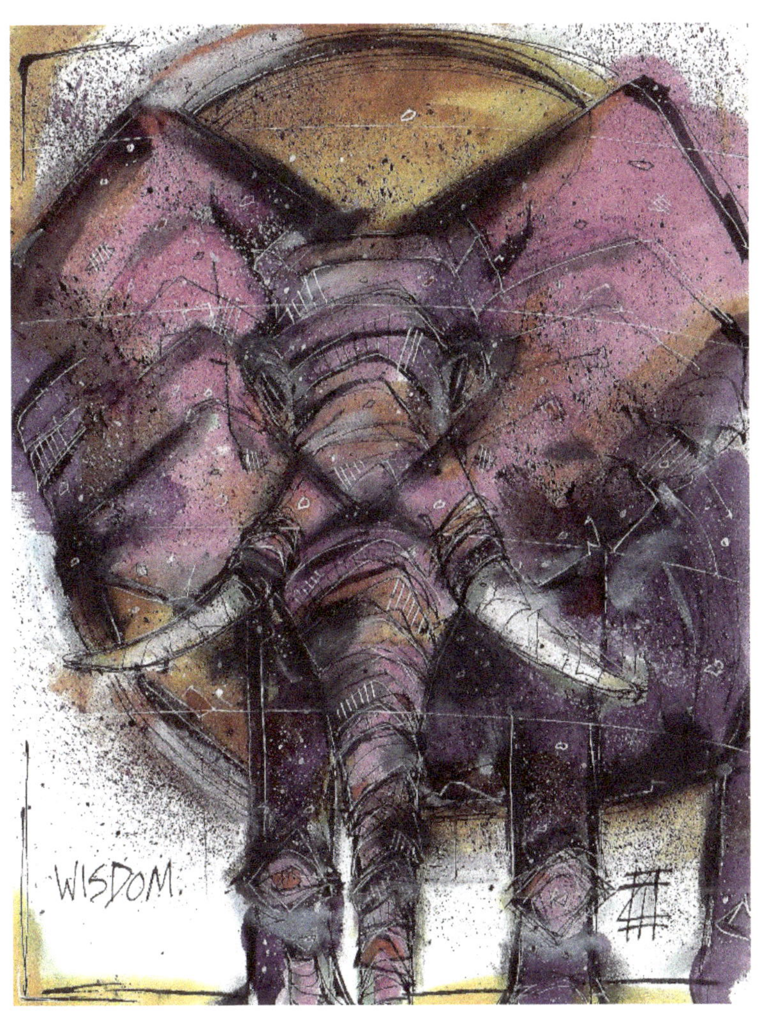
WISDOM.

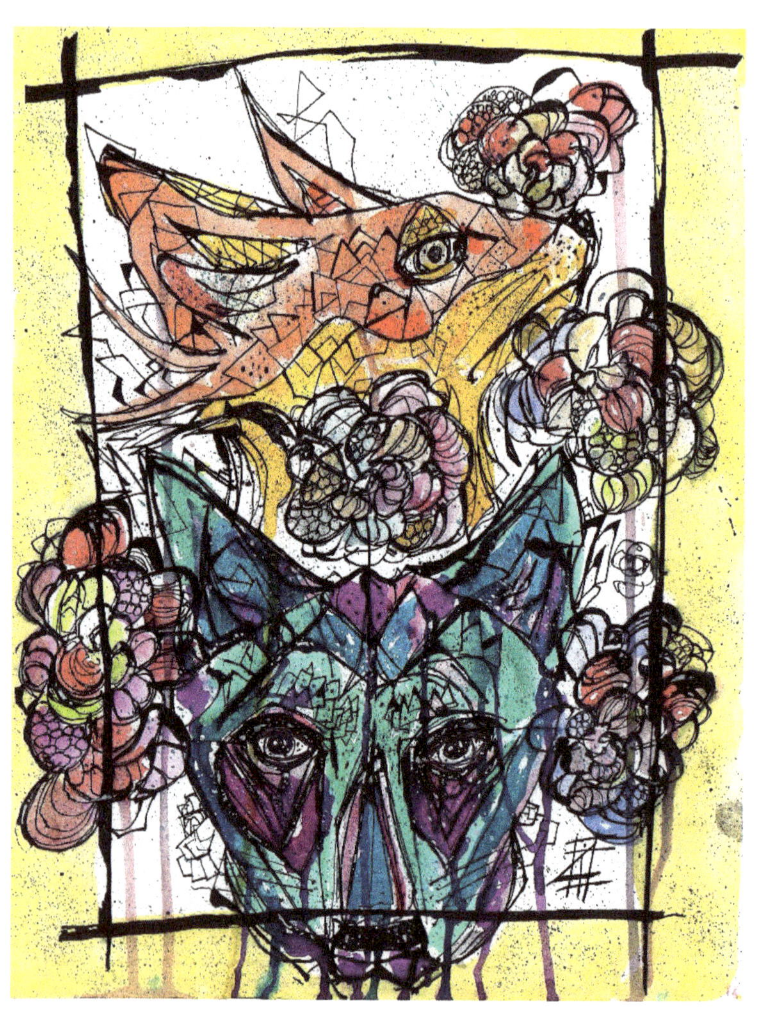

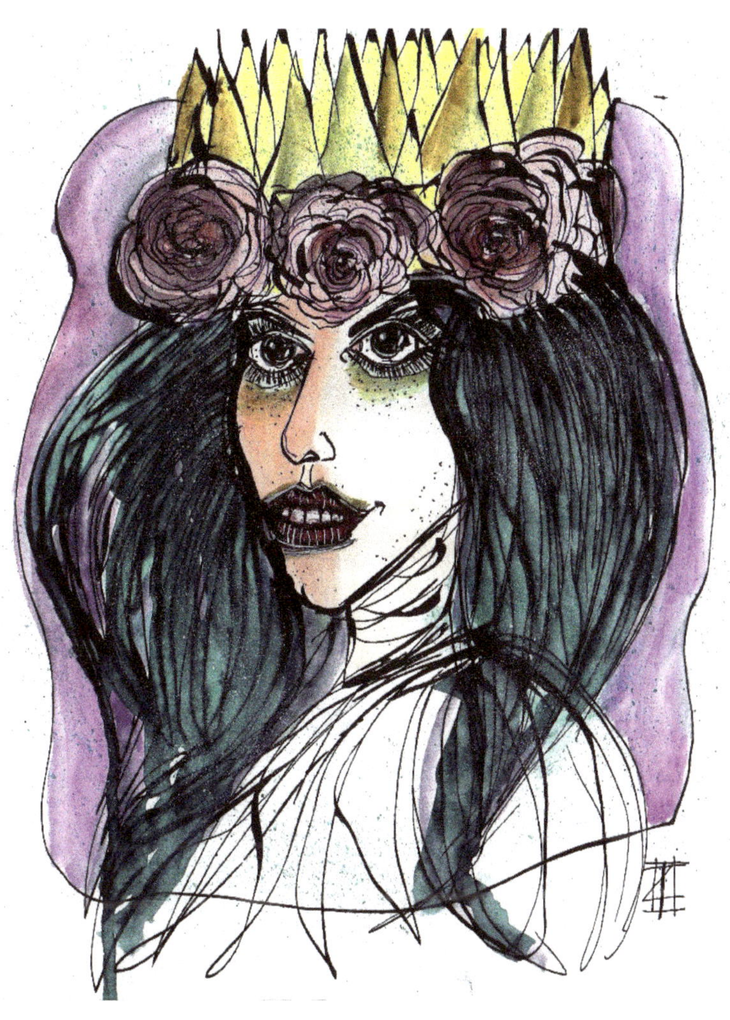

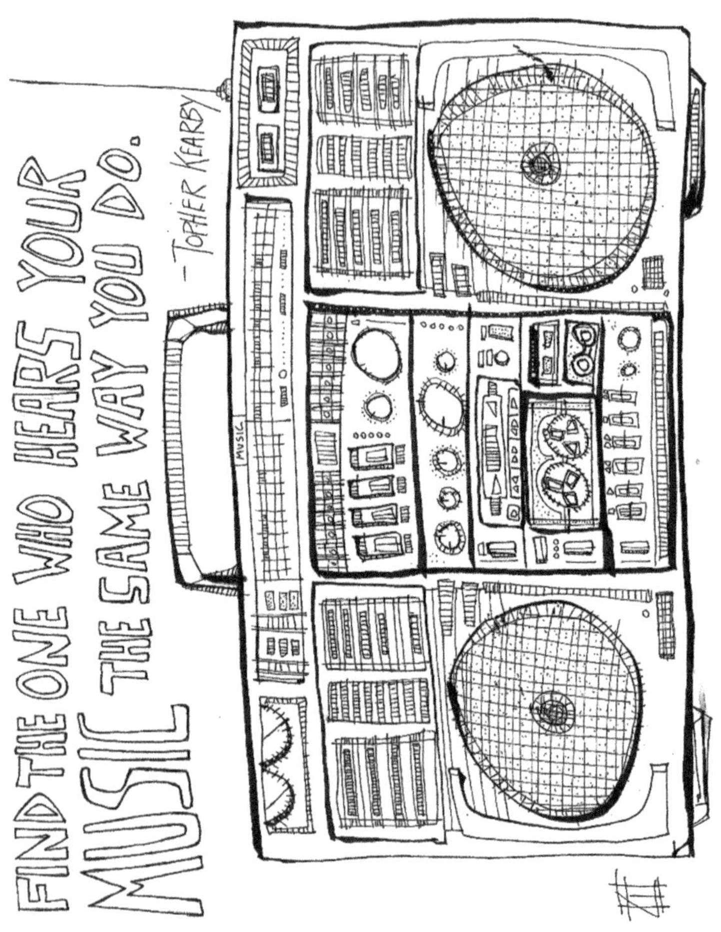
FIND THE ONE WHO HEARS YOUR
MUSIC THE SAME WAY YOU DO.
-TOPHER KEARBY
MUSIC

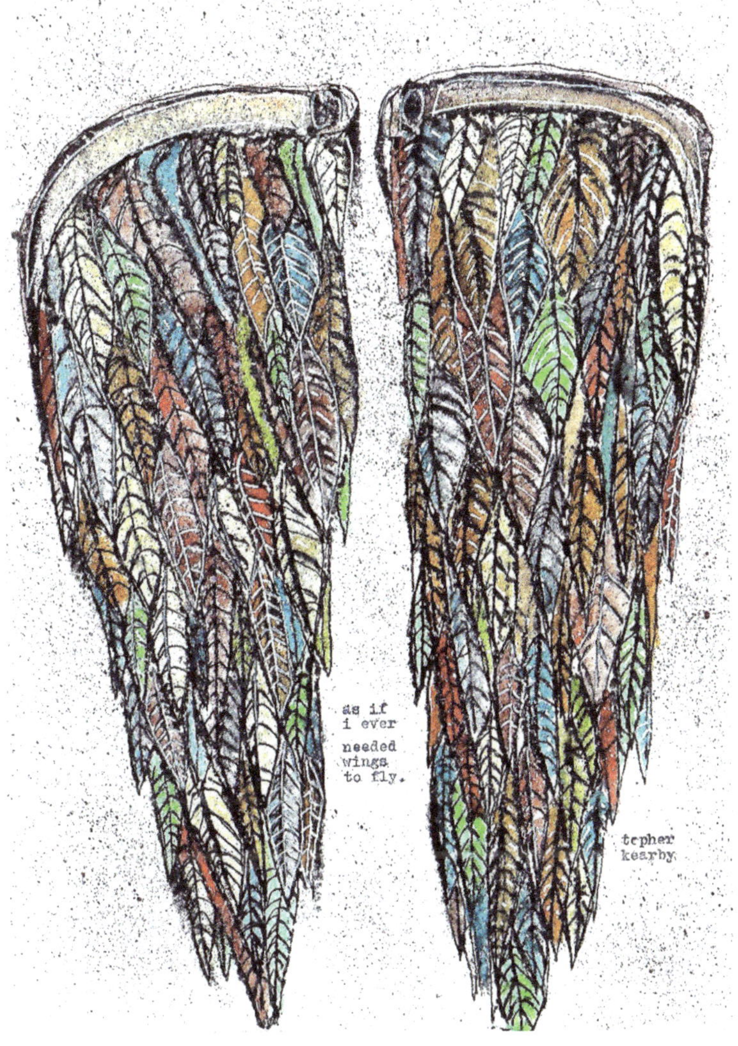
as if
i ever
needed
wings
to fly.
tepher
kearby

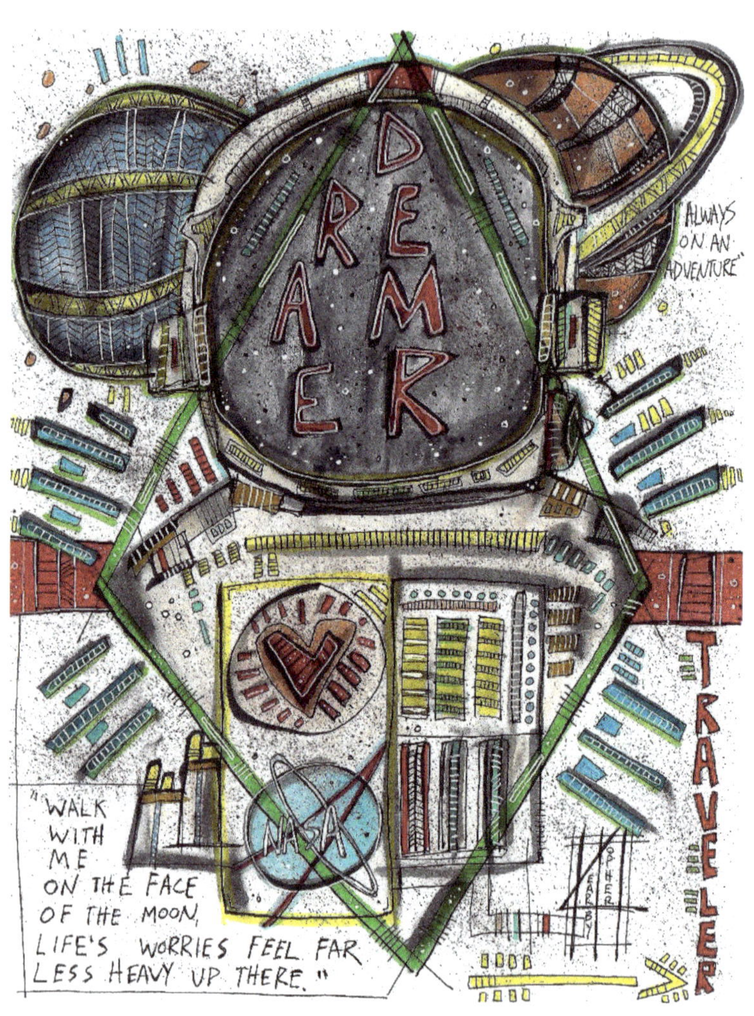
DREAMER
"ALWAYS ON AN ADVENTURE"
TRAVELER
NASA
"WALK WITH ME ON THE FACE OF THE MOON, LIFE'S WORRIES FEEL FAR LESS HEAVY UP THERE."

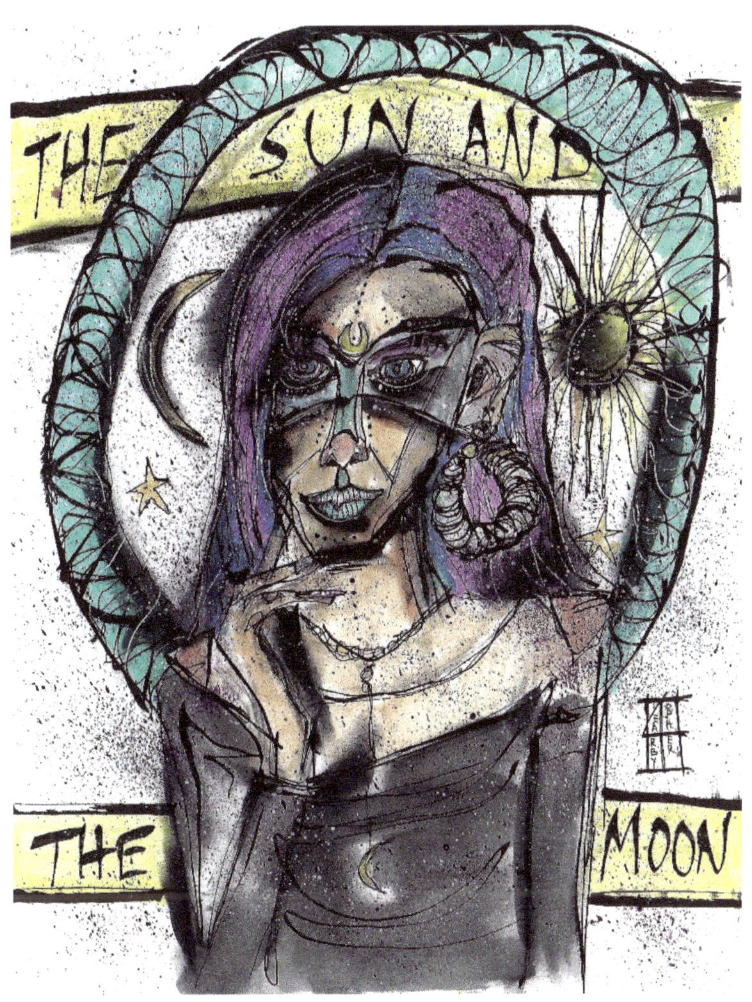
THE SUN AND
THE MOON

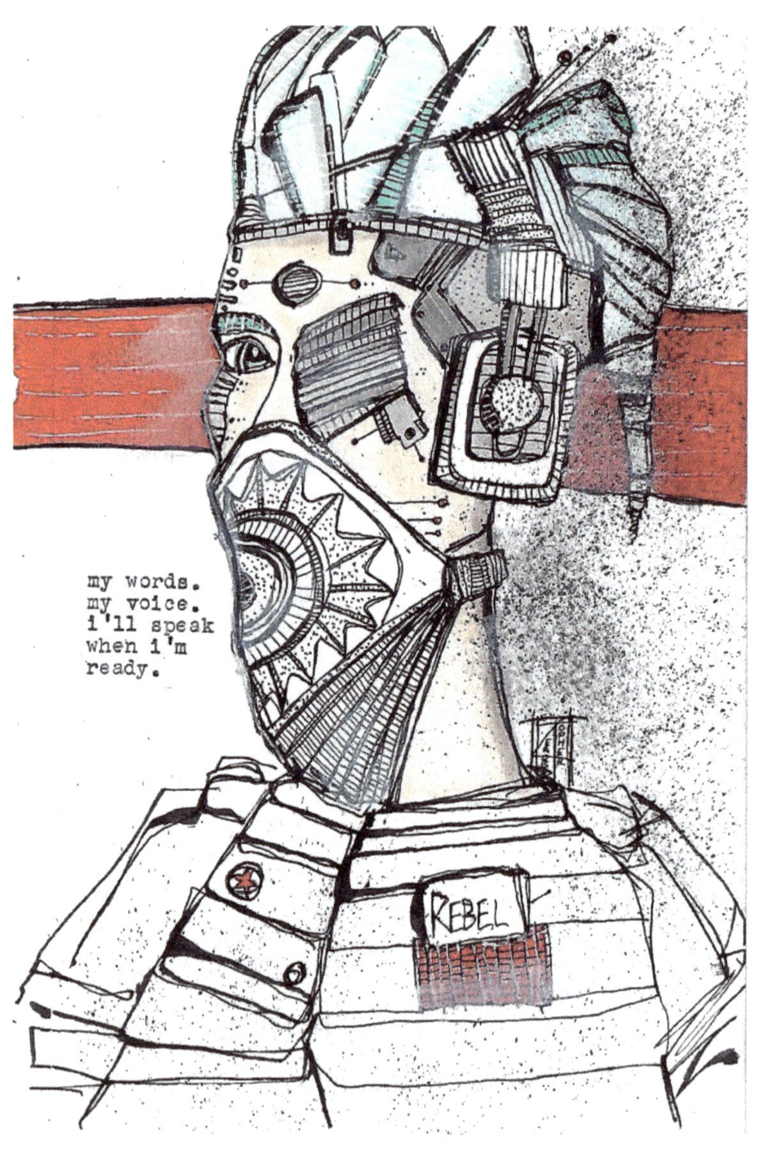
my words.
my voice.
i'll speak
when i'm
ready.
REBEL

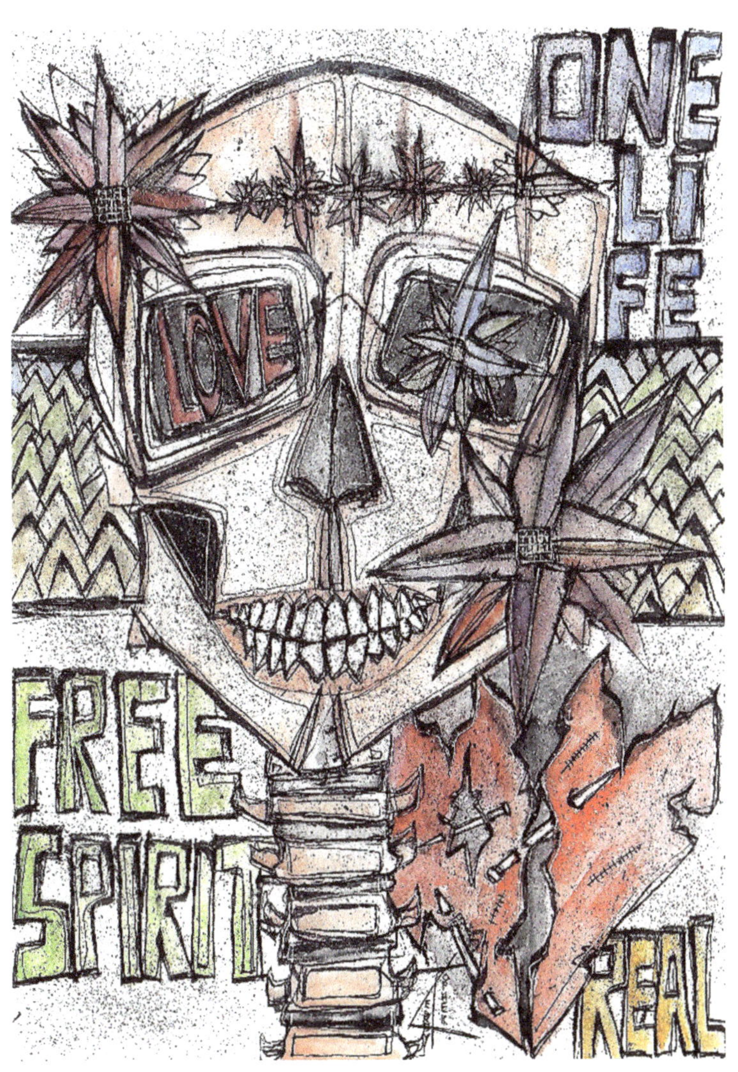
ONE
LI
FE
LOVE
FREE
SPIRIT
REAL

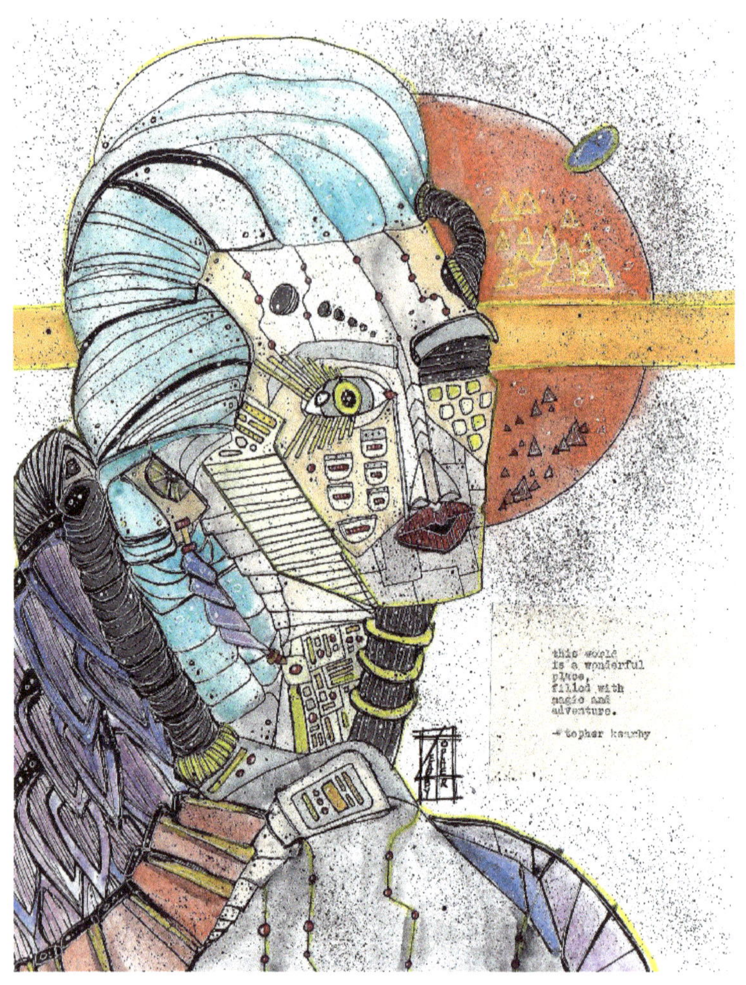
this world
is a wonderful
place,
filled with
magic and
adventure.
- topher

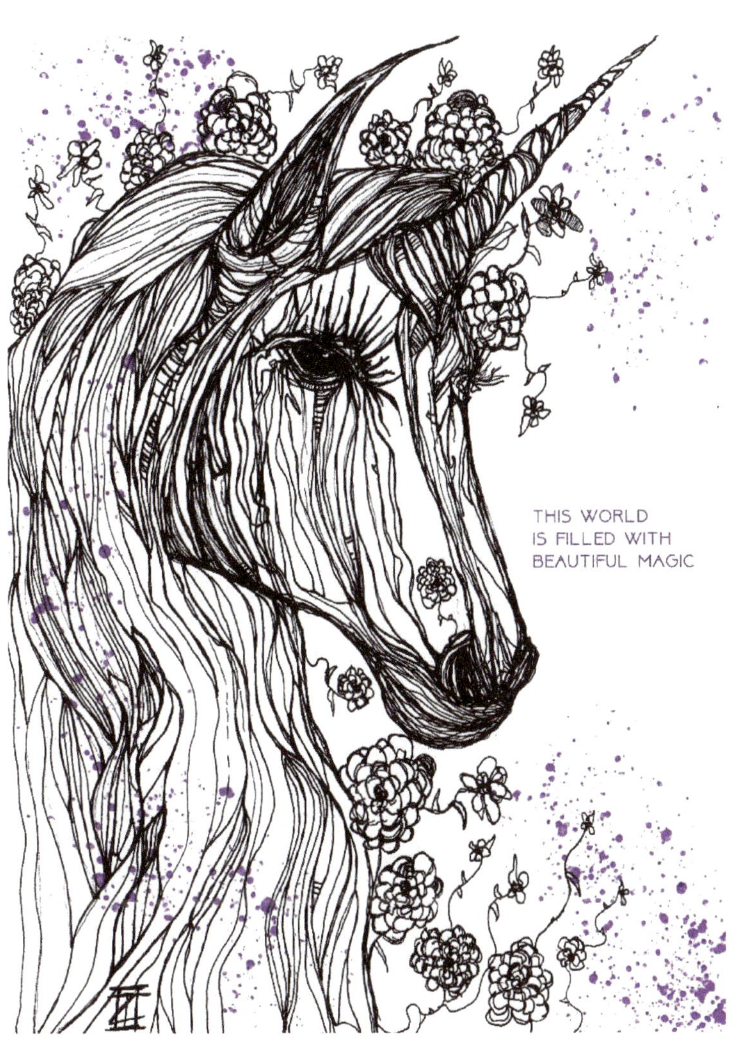
THIS WORLD
IS FILLED WITH
BEAUTIFUL MAGIC

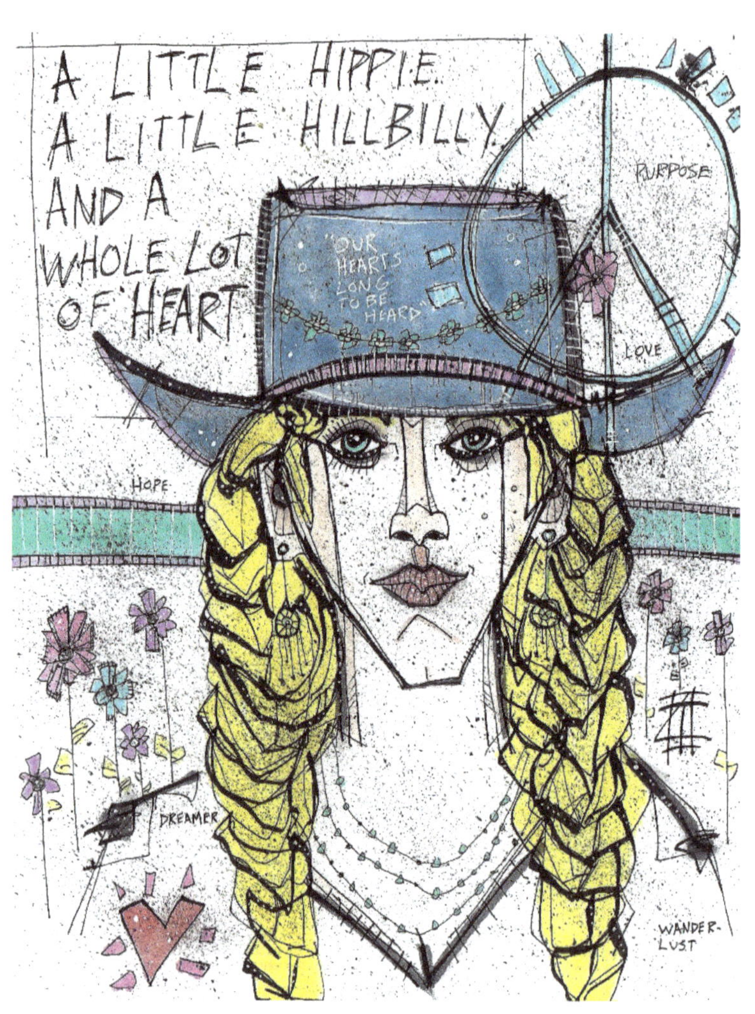
A LITTLE HIPPIE
A LITTLE HILLBILLY
AND A
WHOLE LOT
OF HEART
"OUR HEARTS LONG TO BE HEARD"
PURPOSE
LOVE
HOPE
DREAMER
WANDER-LUST

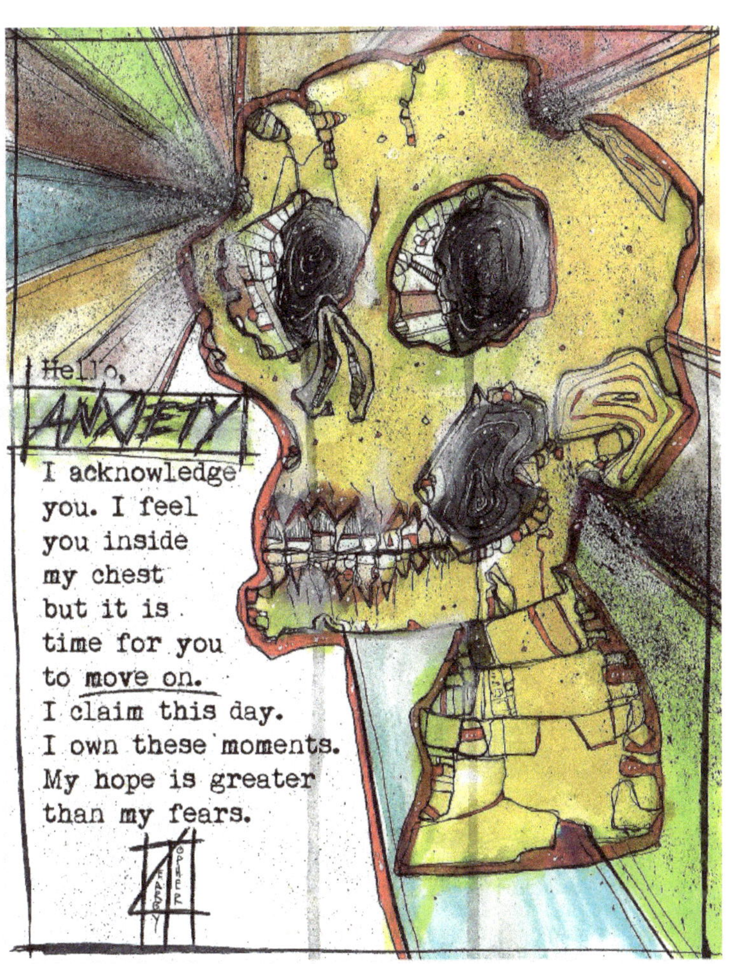
Hello,
ANXIETY
I acknowledge
you. I feel
you inside
my chest
but it is
time for you
to move on.
I claim this day.
I own these moments.
My hope is greater
than my fears.

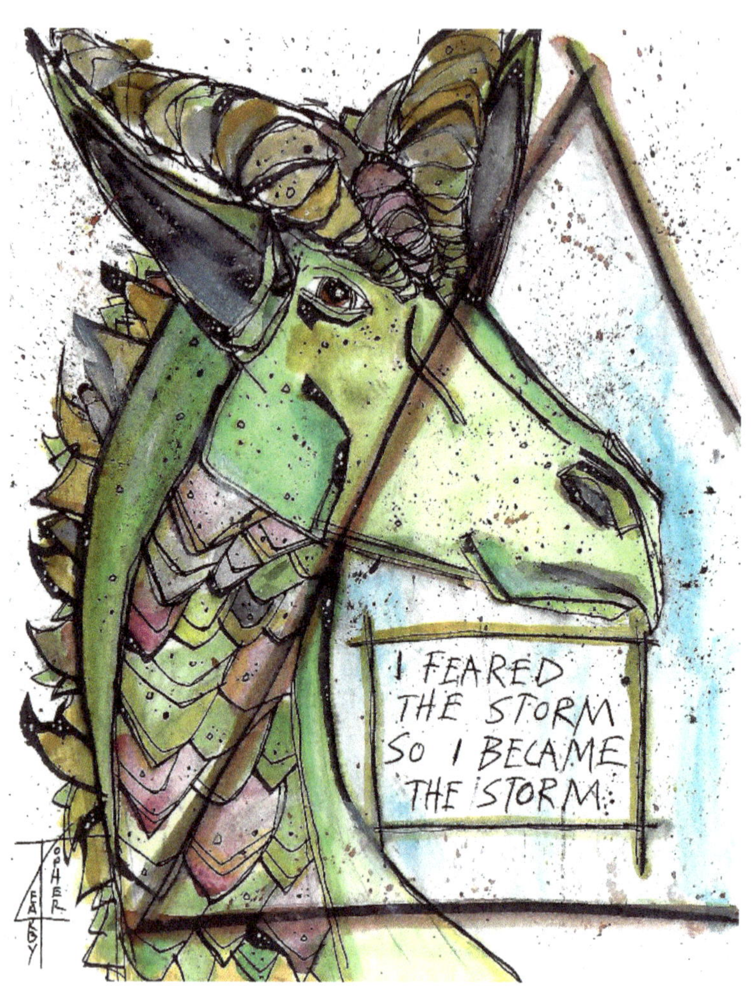
I FEARED
THE STORM
SO I BECAME
THE STORM.

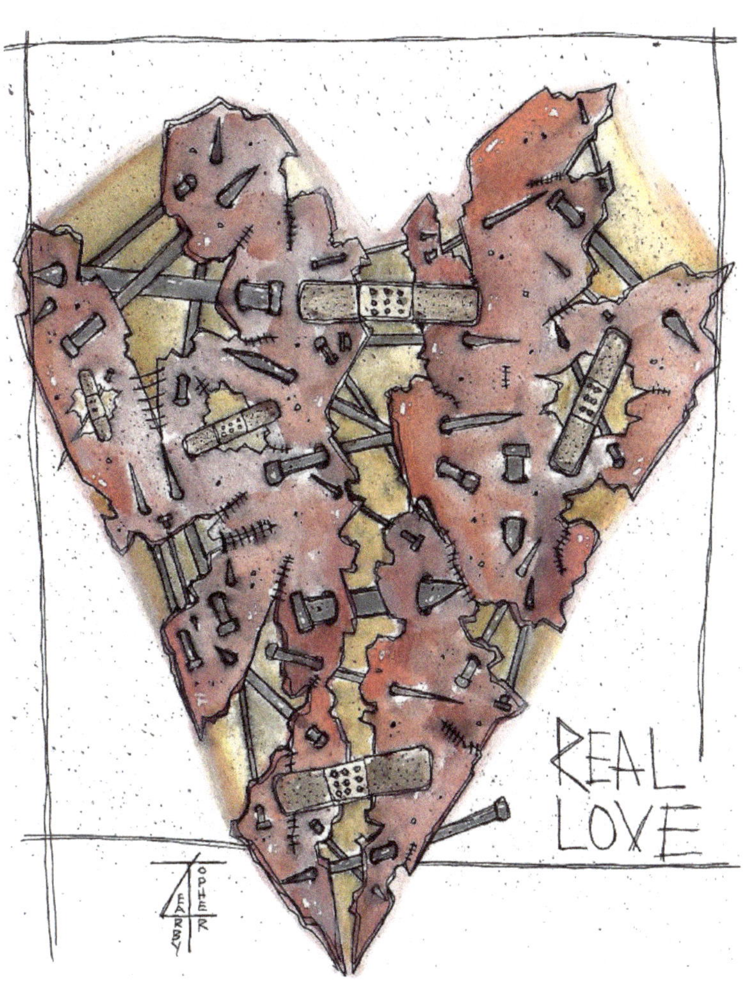
REAL
LOVE

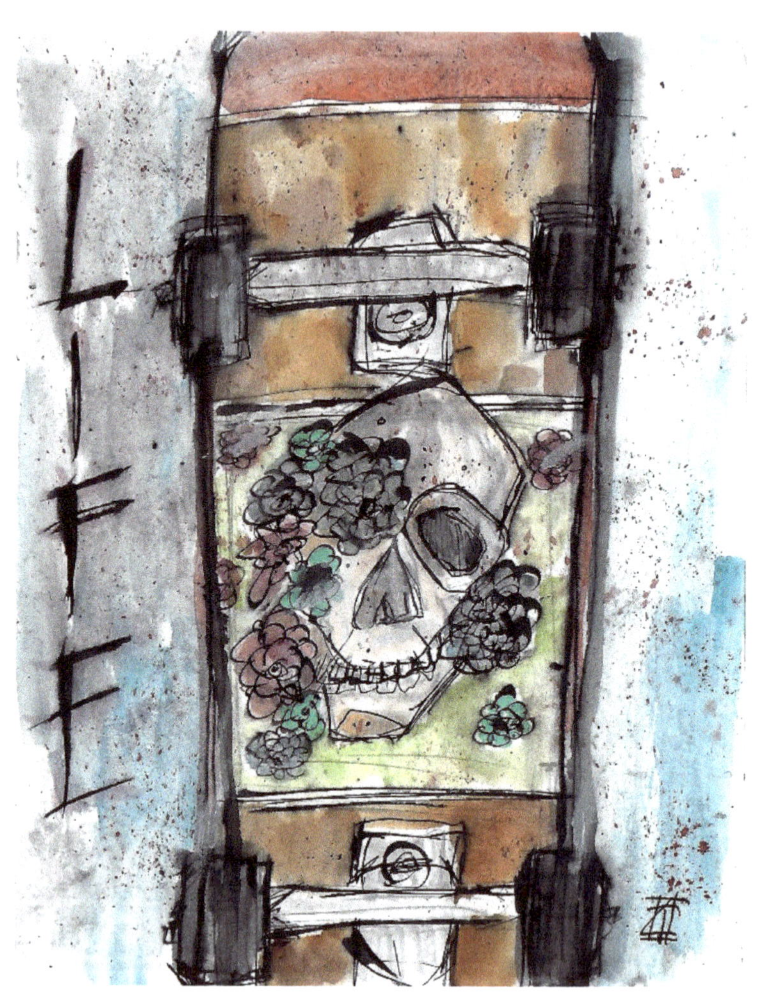
LIFE

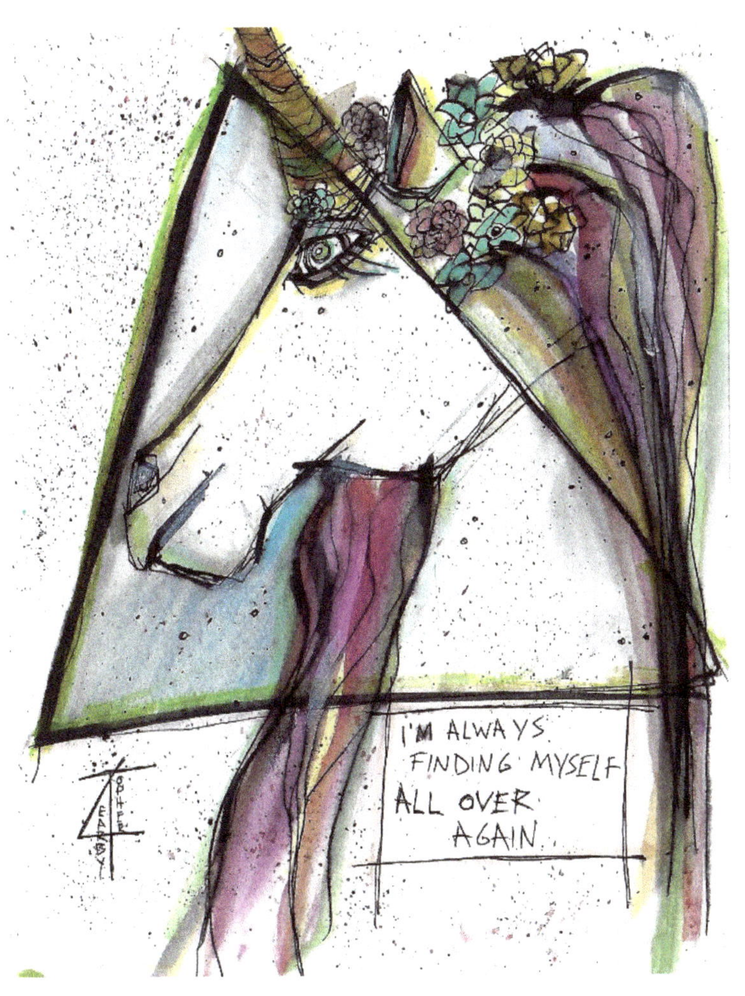
I'M ALWAYS
FINDING MYSELF
ALL OVER
AGAIN

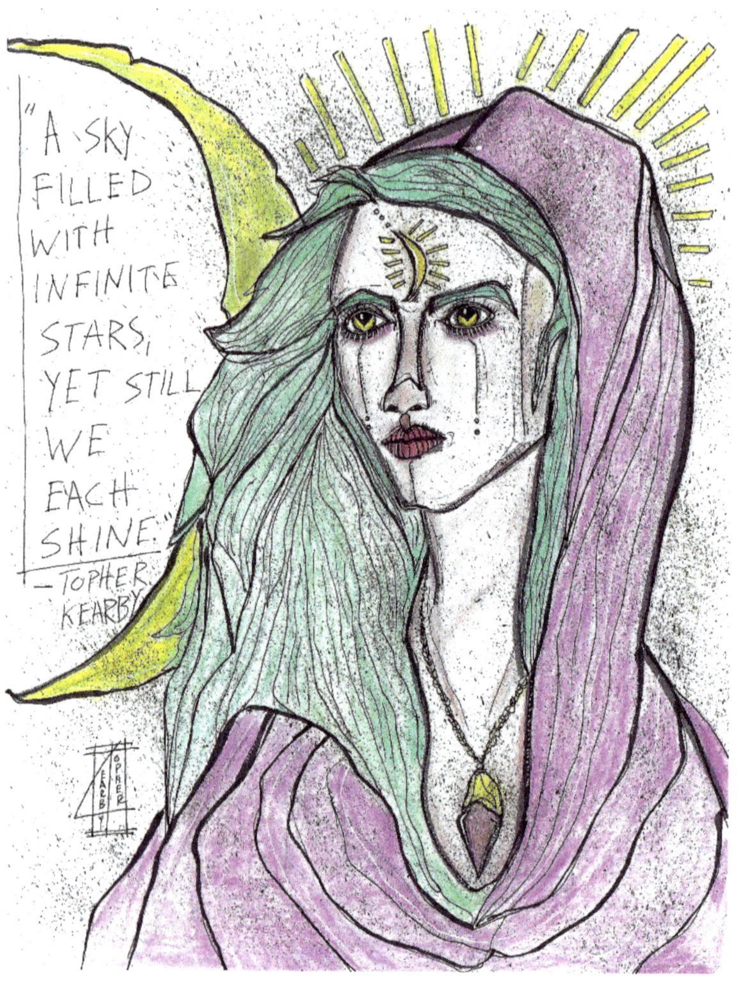
"A SKY
FILLED
WITH
INFINITE
STARS,
YET STILL
WE
EACH
SHINE."
-TOPHER
KEARBY

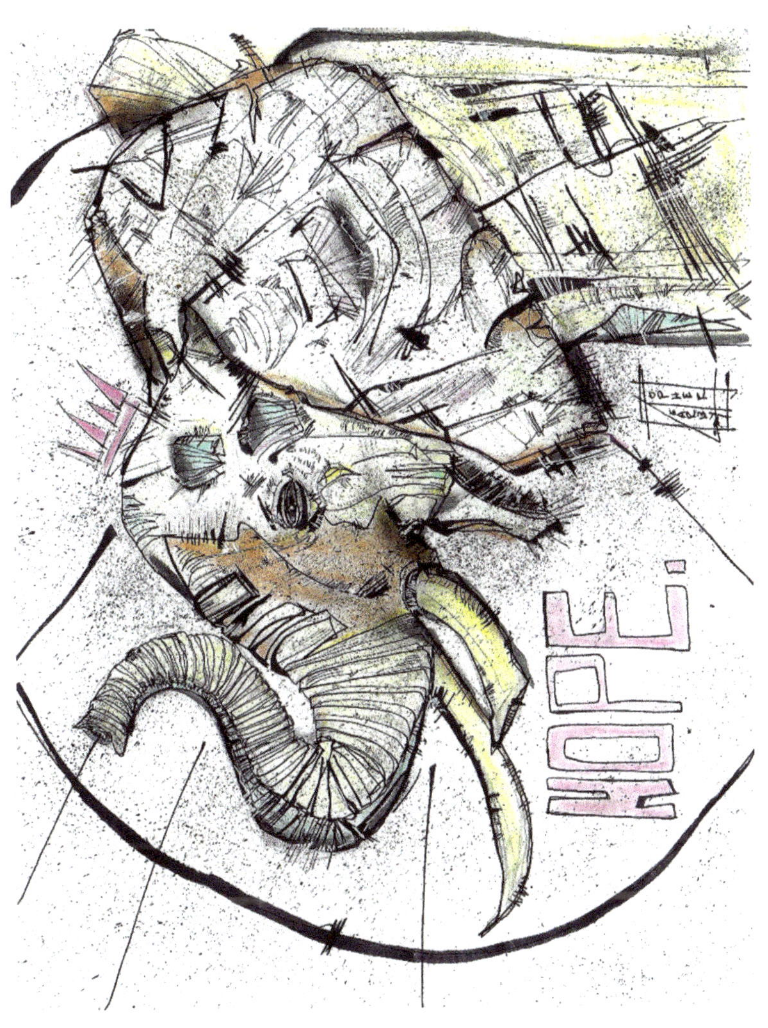
HOPE.

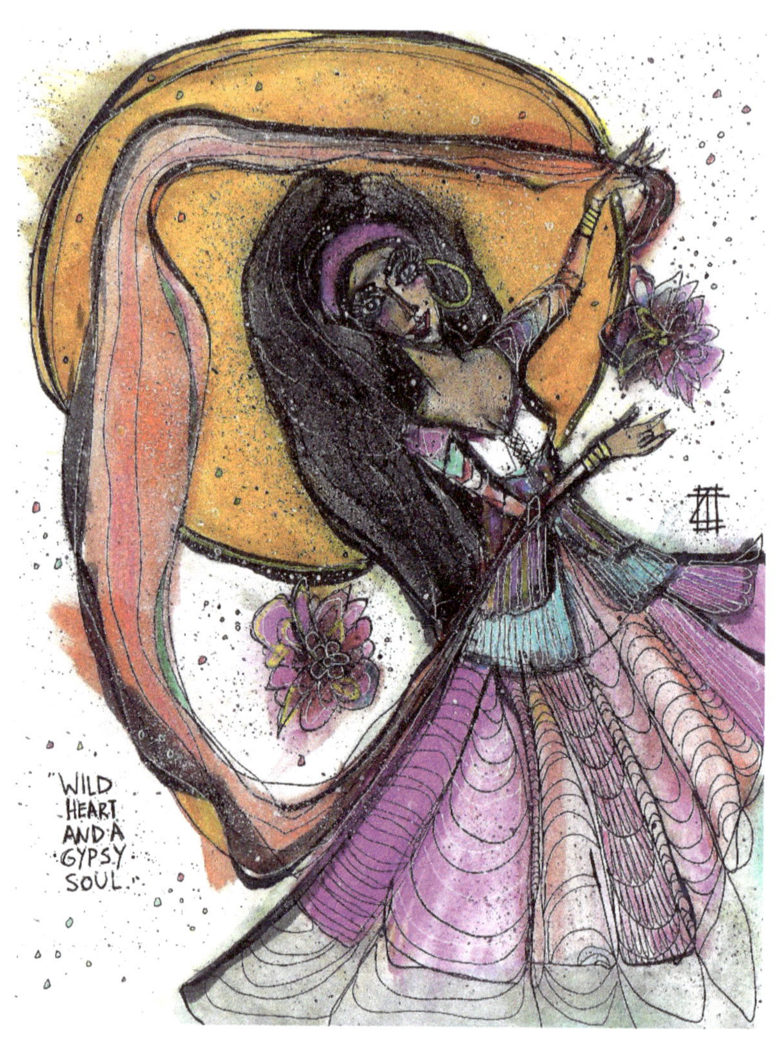
"WILD HEART AND A GYPSY SOUL."

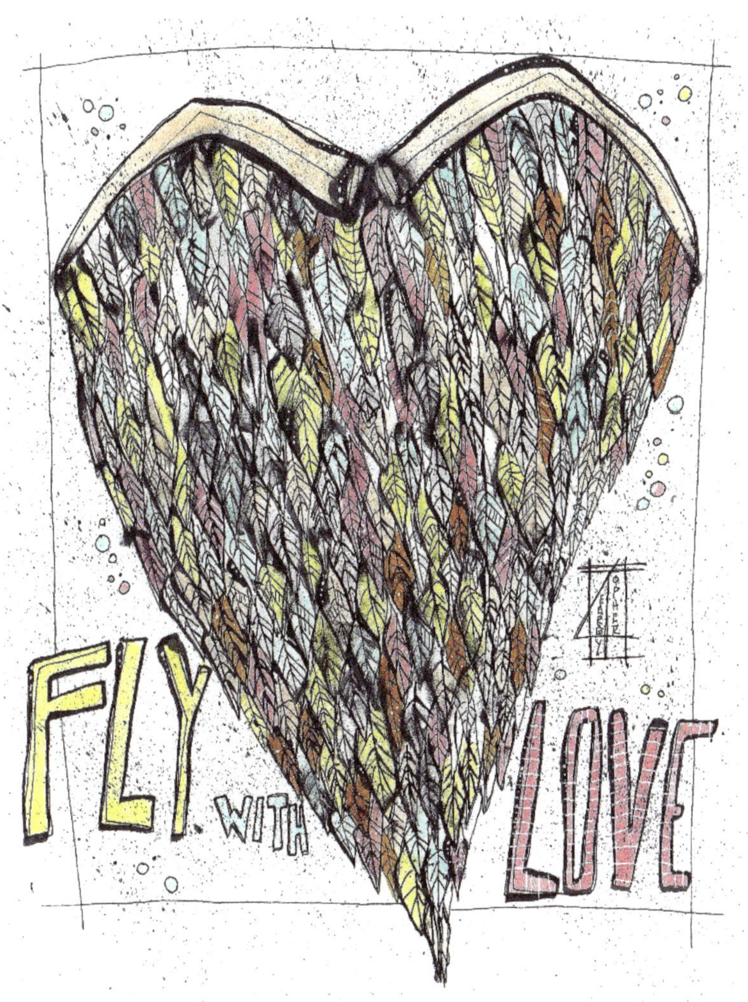
FLY
WITH
LOVE

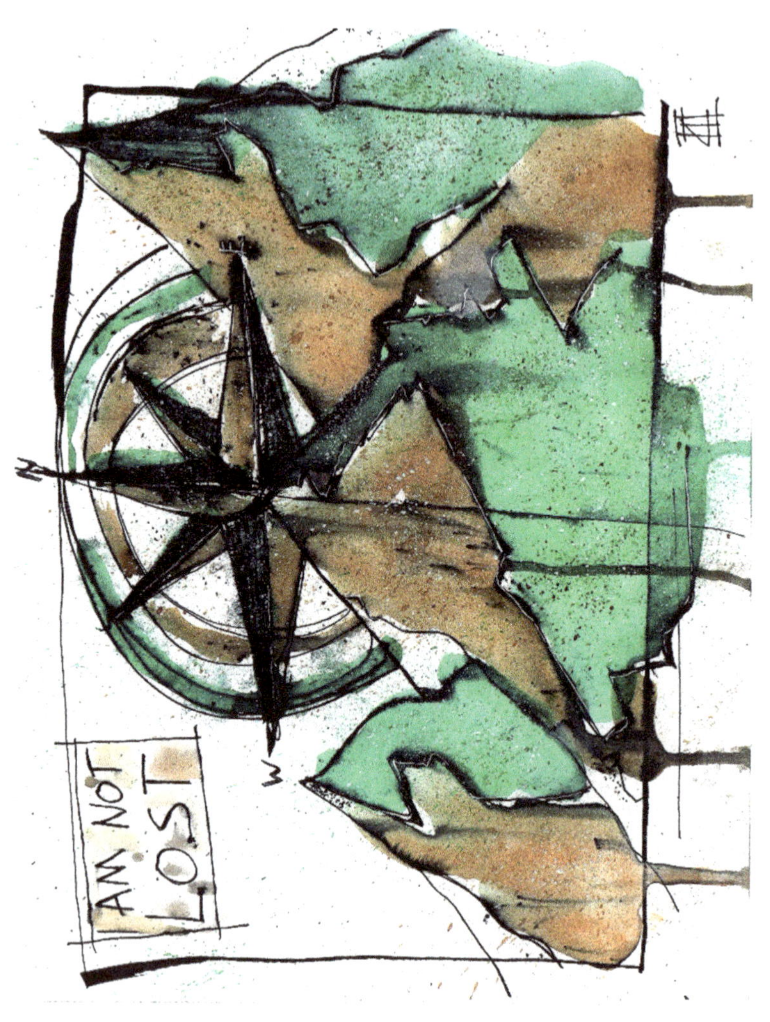
AM NOT
LOST

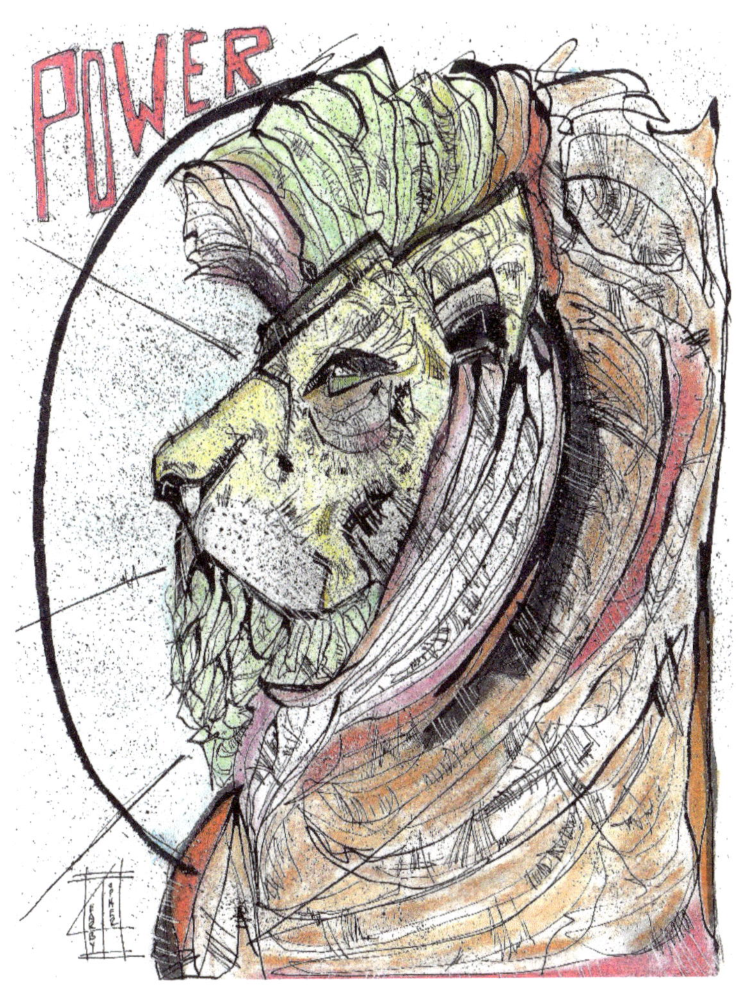
POWER

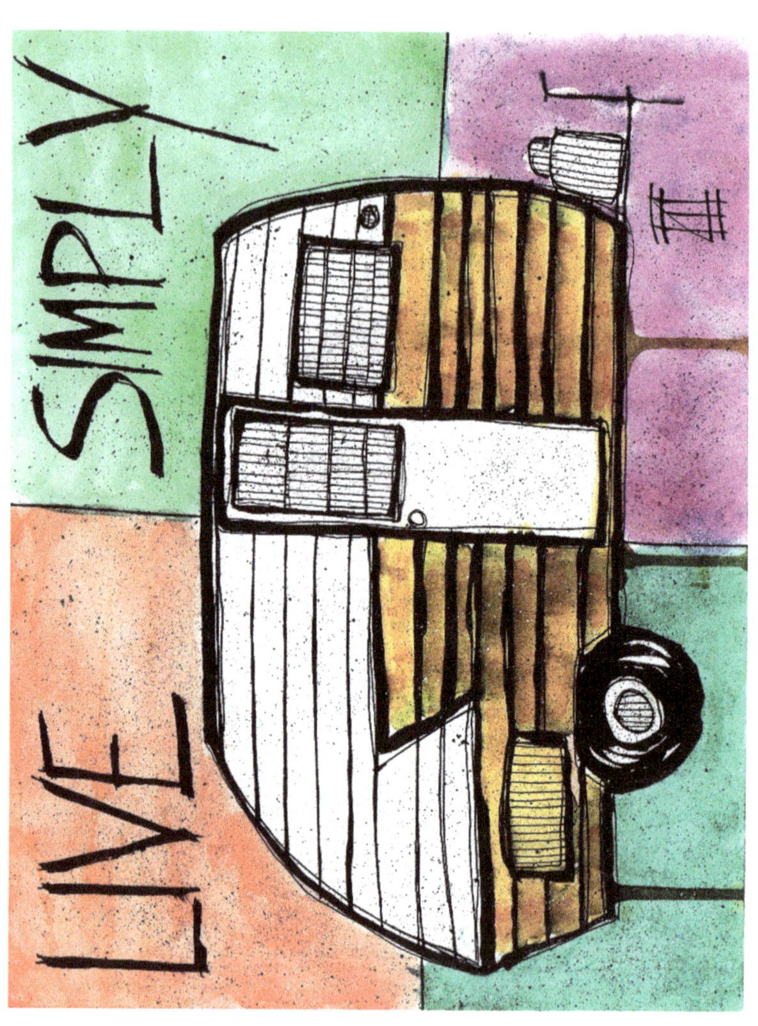
LIVE SIMPLY

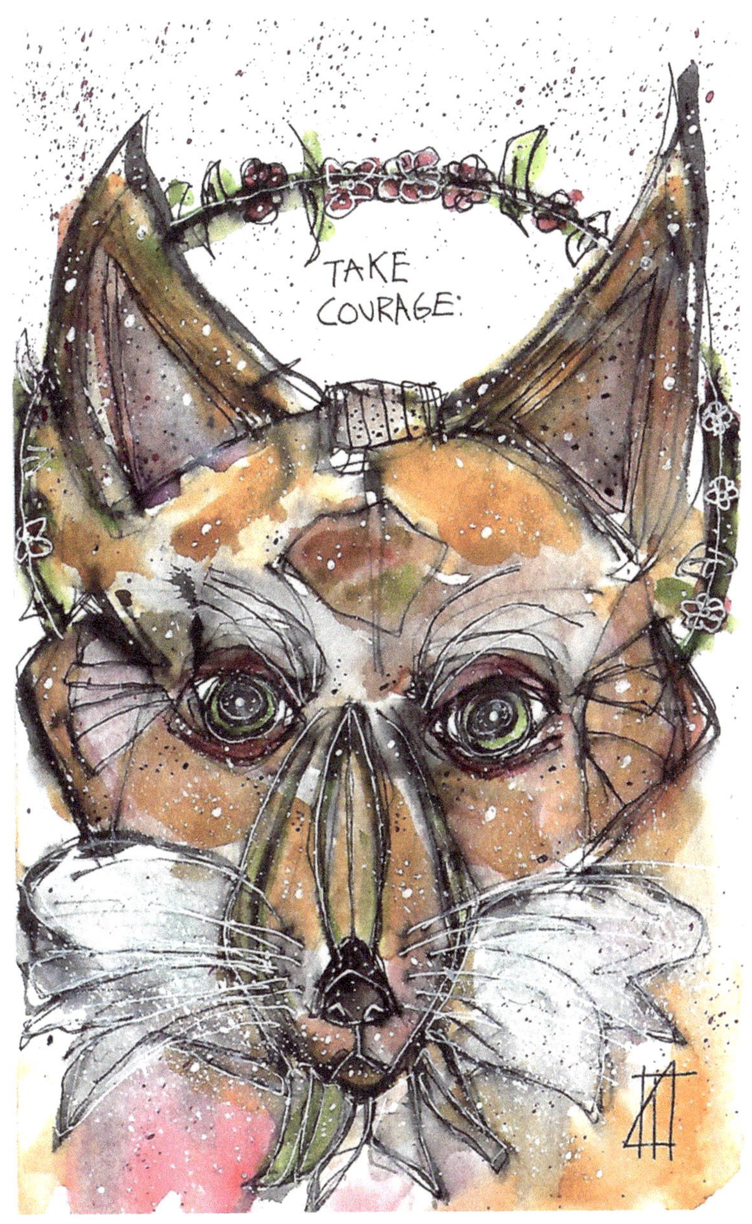
TAKE
COURAGE:

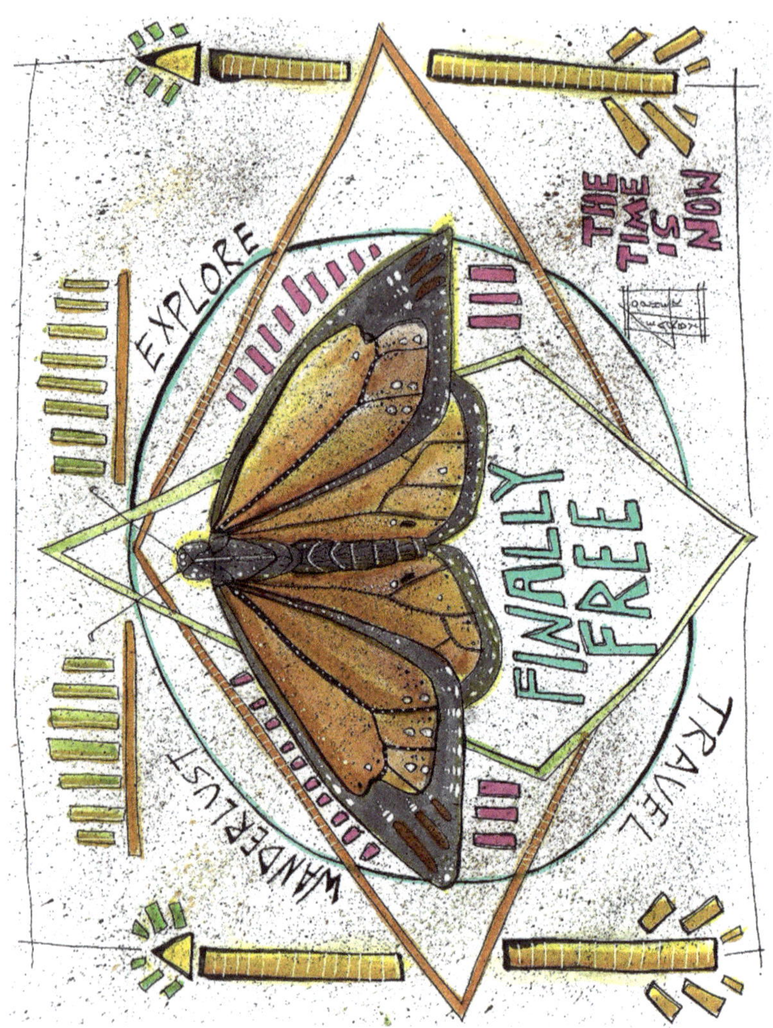
EXPLORE
WANDERLUST
FINALLY FREE
TRAVEL
THE TIME IS NOW

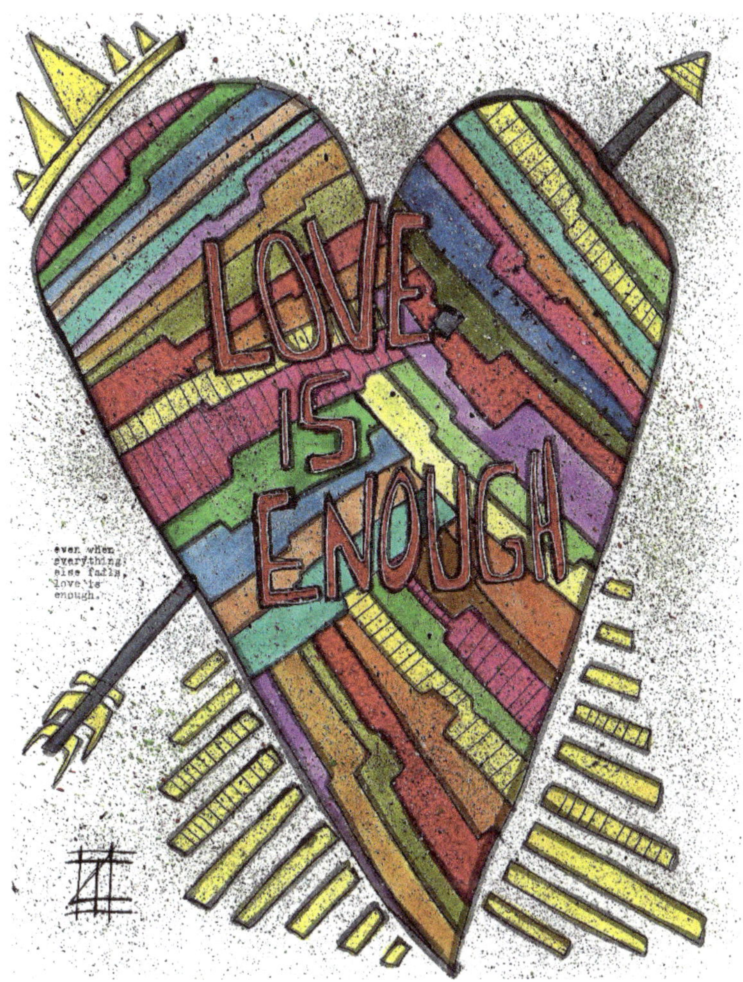
LOVE IS ENOUGH
even when
everything
else fails,
love is
enough.

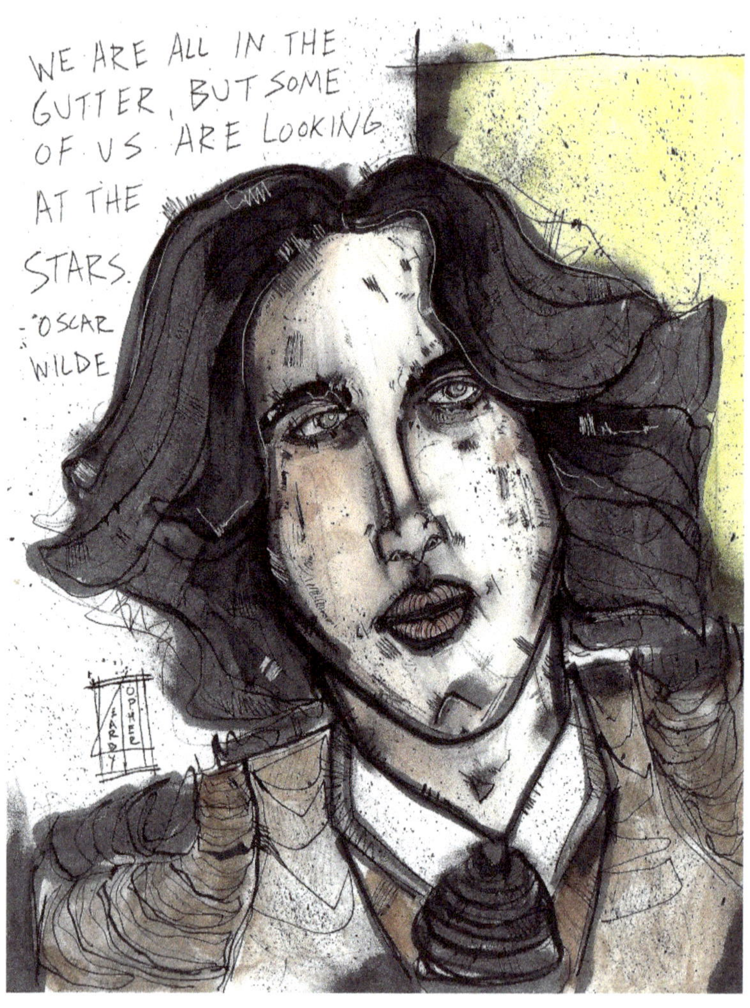
WE ARE ALL IN THE
GUTTER, BUT SOME
OF US ARE LOOKING
AT THE
STARS.
-OSCAR
WILDE

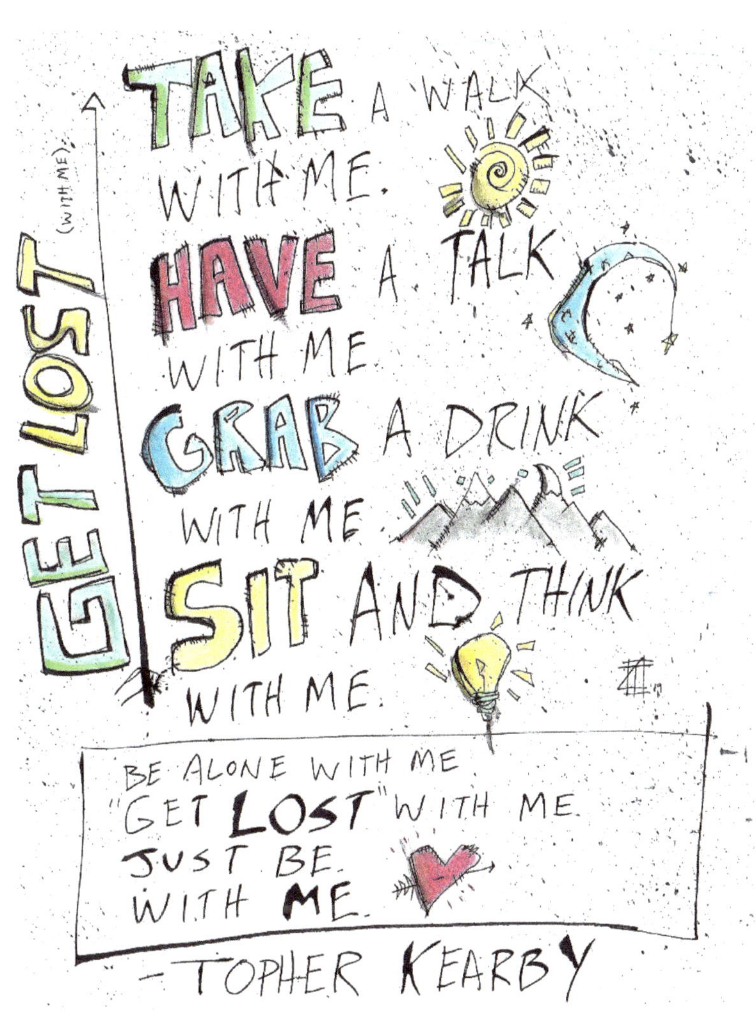
GET LOST (WITH ME)
TAKE A WALK
WITH ME.
HAVE A TALK
WITH ME
GRAB A DRINK
WITH ME
SIT AND THINK
WITH ME.
BE ALONE WITH ME
"GET LOST" WITH ME.
JUST BE
WITH ME
- TOPHER KEARBY

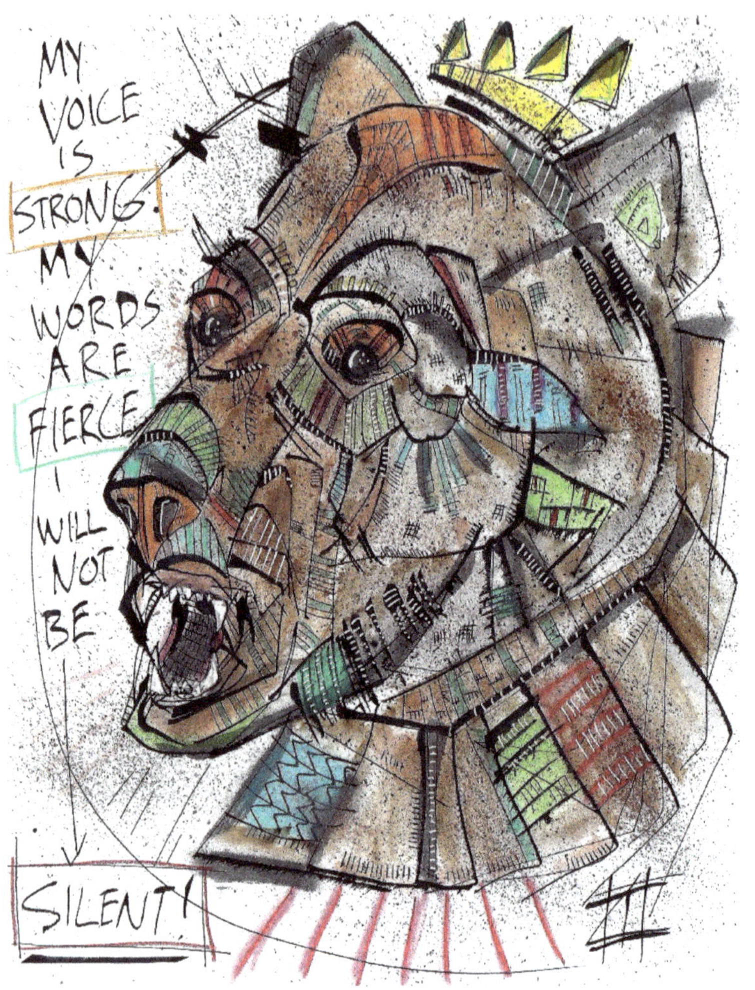
MY
VOICE
IS
STRONG.
MY
WORDS
ARE
FIERCE
I
WILL
NOT
BE
SILENT!

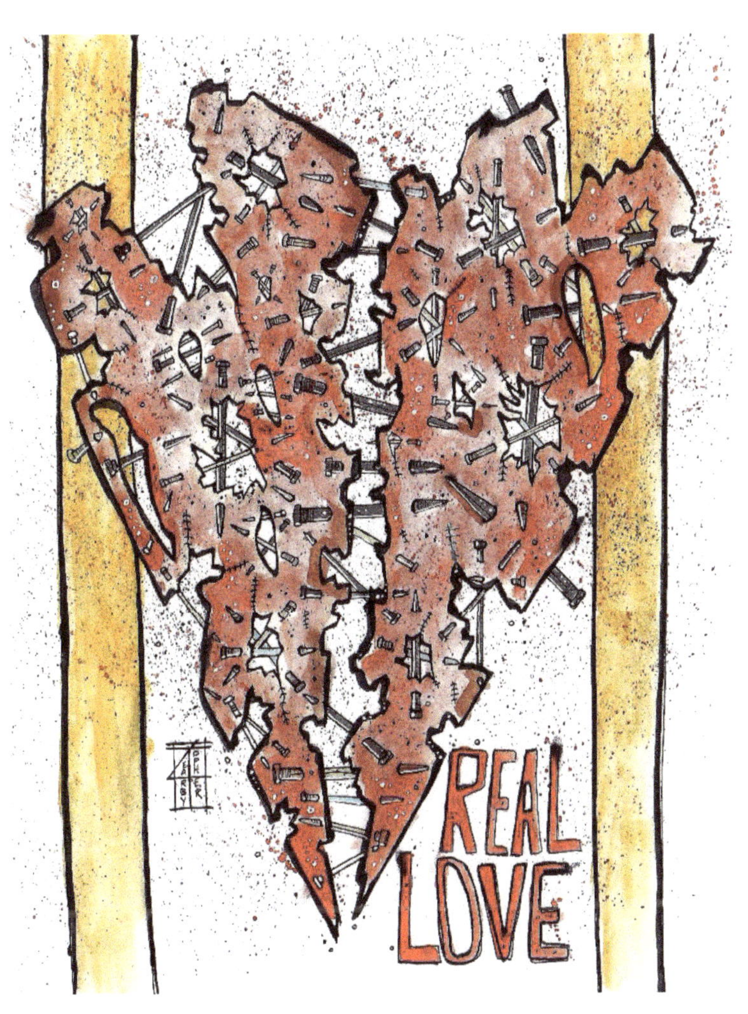
REAL
LOVE

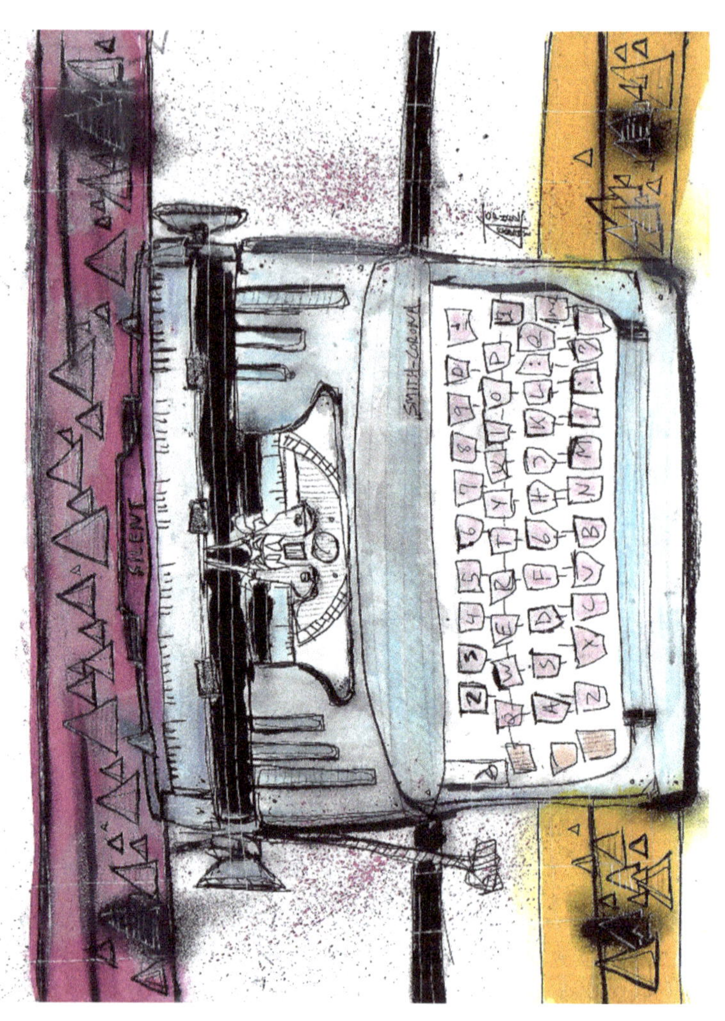
SILENT
SMITH-CORONA

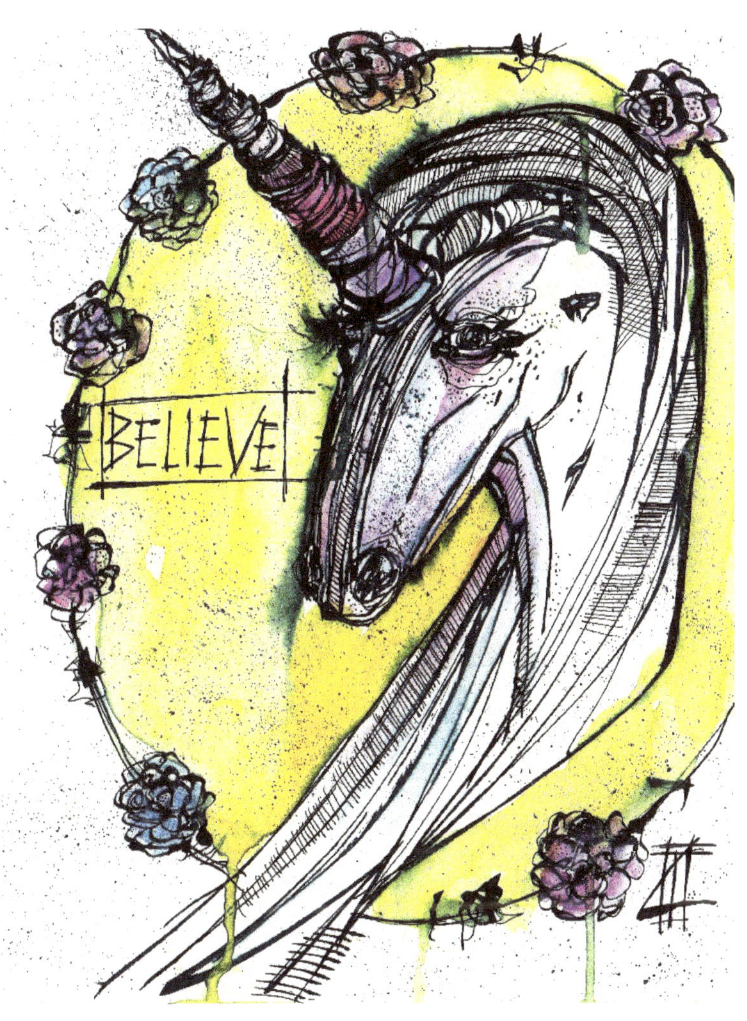
BELIEVE

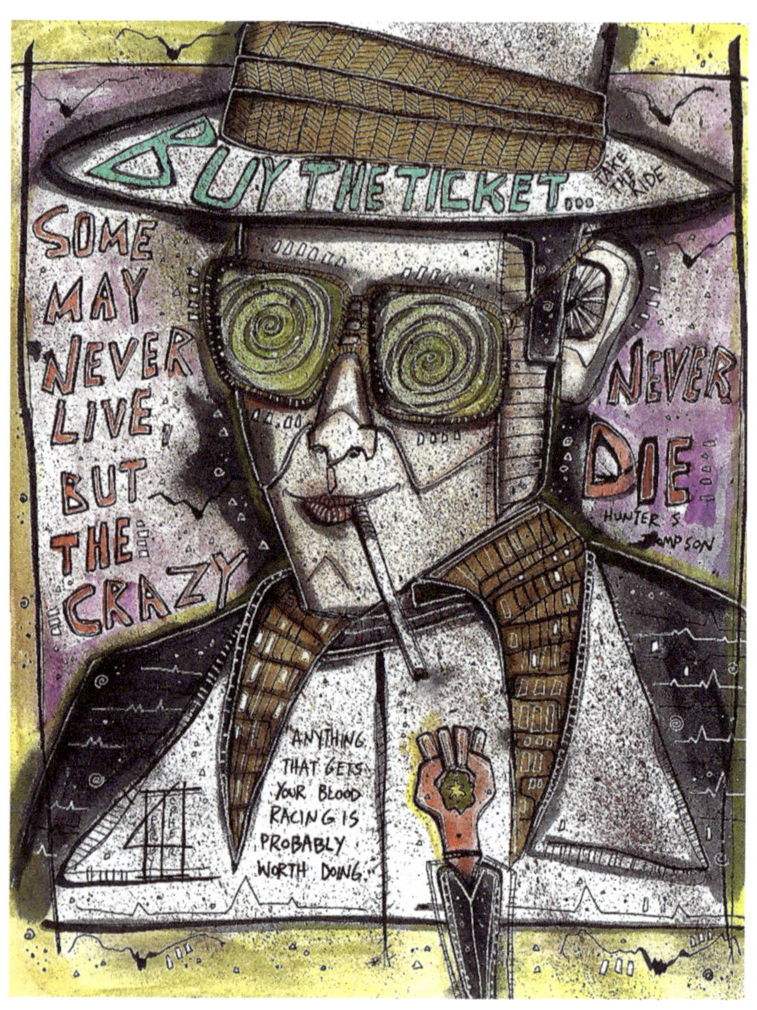
BUY THE TICKET...
TAKE THE RIDE
SOME MAY NEVER LIVE, BUT THE CRAZY
NEVER DIE
HUNTER S
ANYTHING THAT GETS YOUR BLOOD RACING IS PROBABLY WORTH DOING.

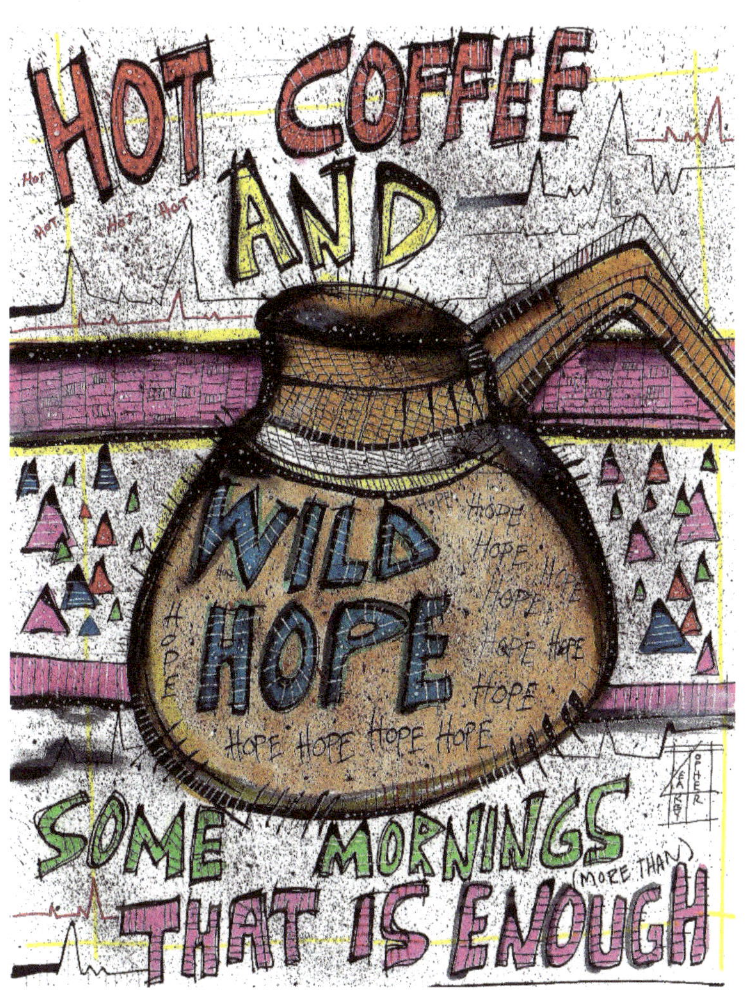
HOT COFFEE
AND
WILD
HOPE
SOME MORNINGS
(MORE THAN)
THAT IS ENOUGH

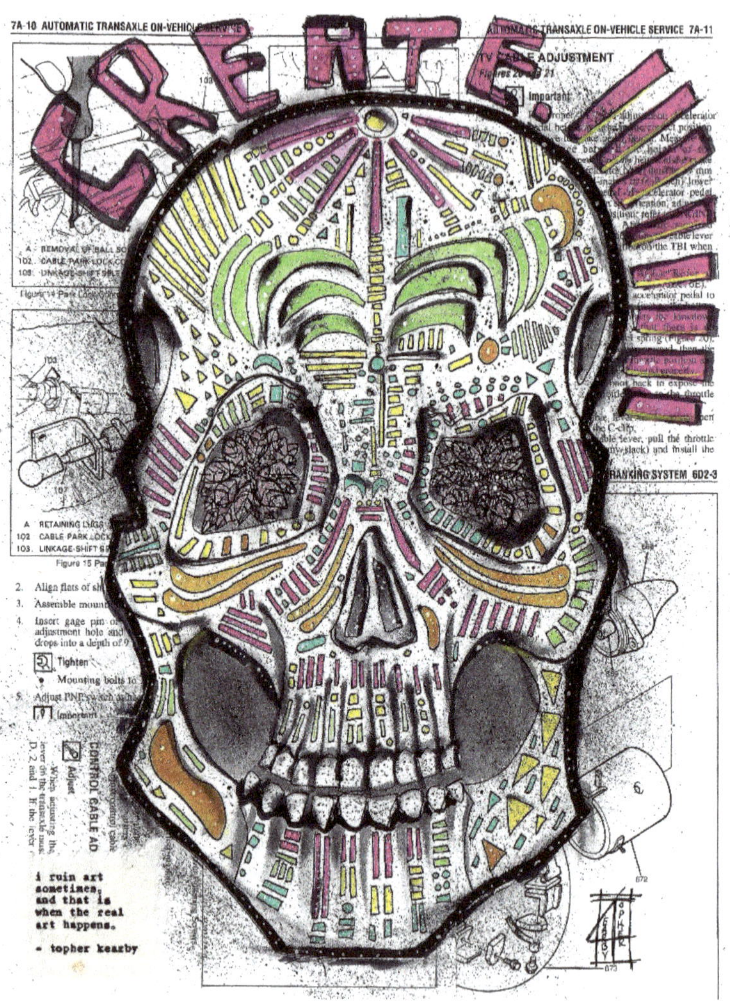
CREATE!!!
i ruin art
sometimes,
and that is
when the real
art happens.
- topher kearby

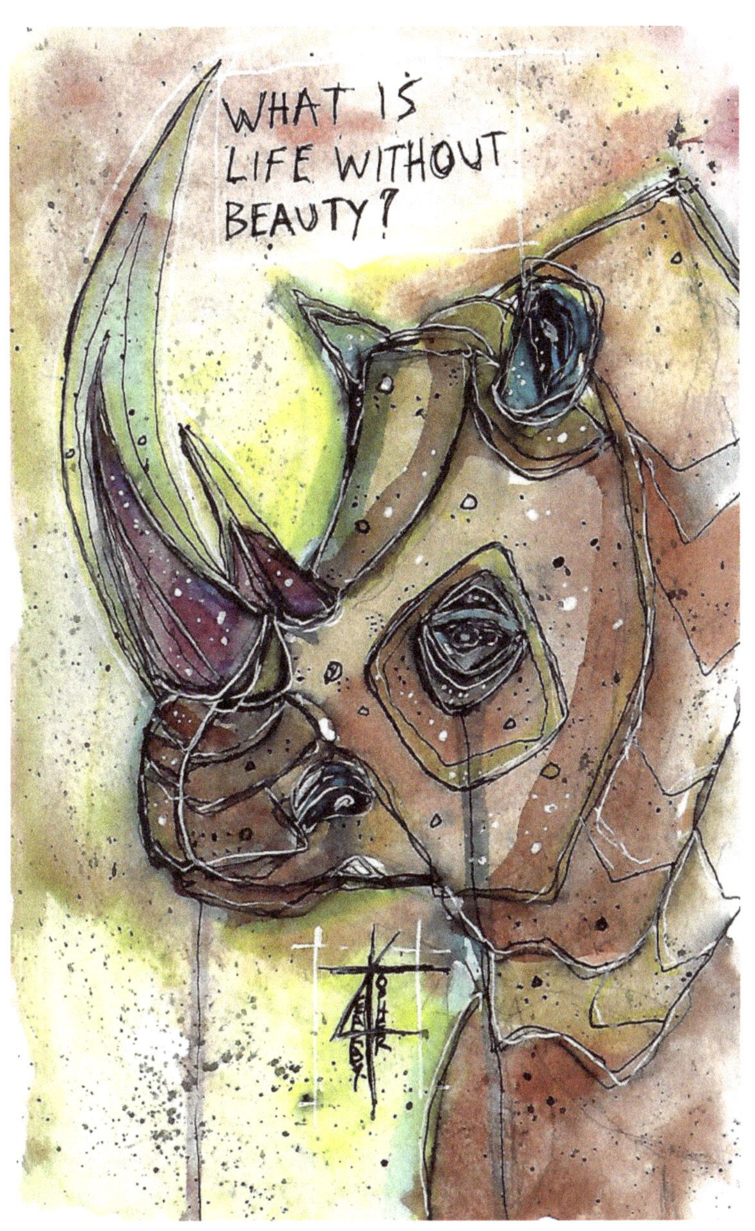
WHAT IS
LIFE WITHOUT
BEAUTY?

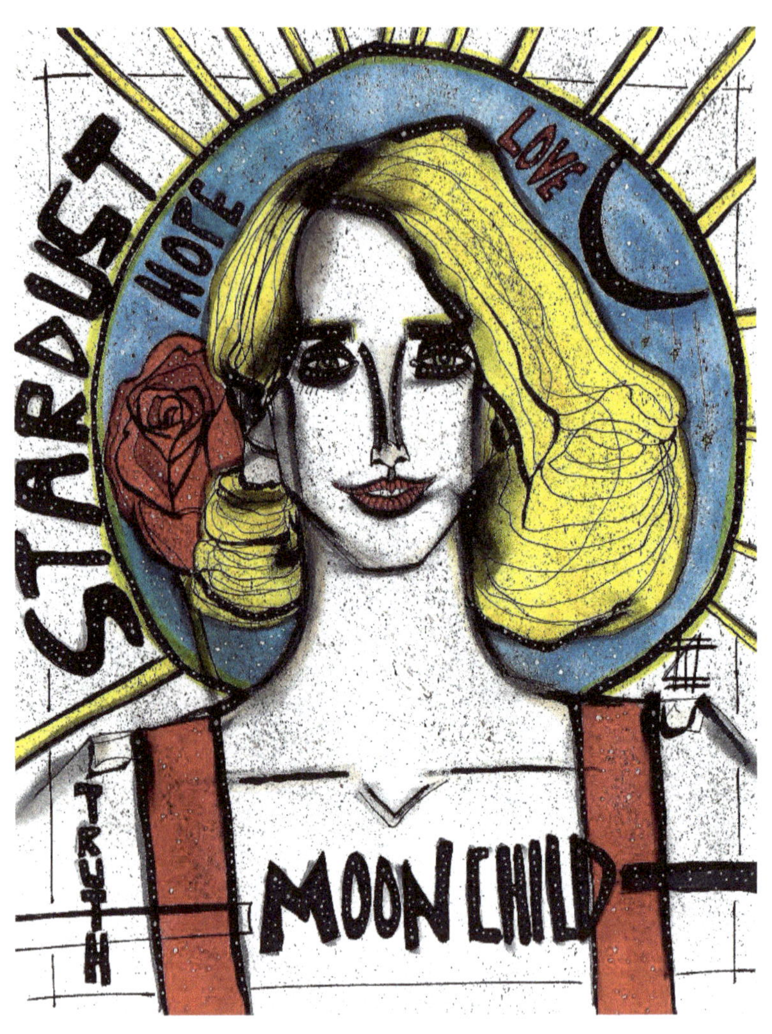
STARDUST
HOPE
LOVE
TRUTH
MOONCHILD

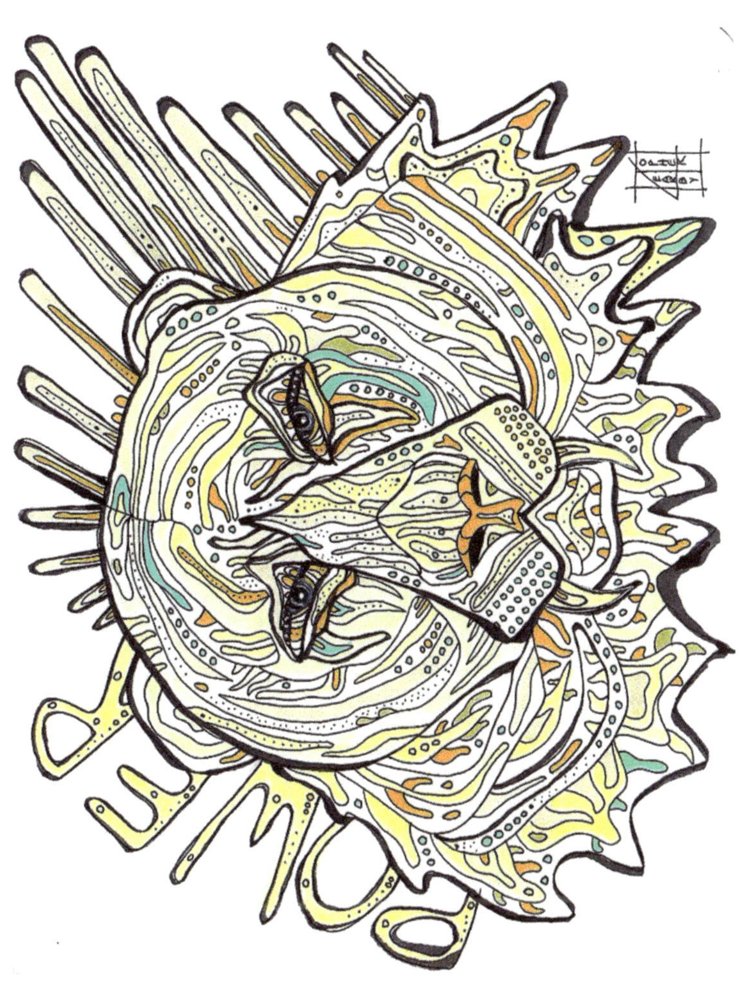

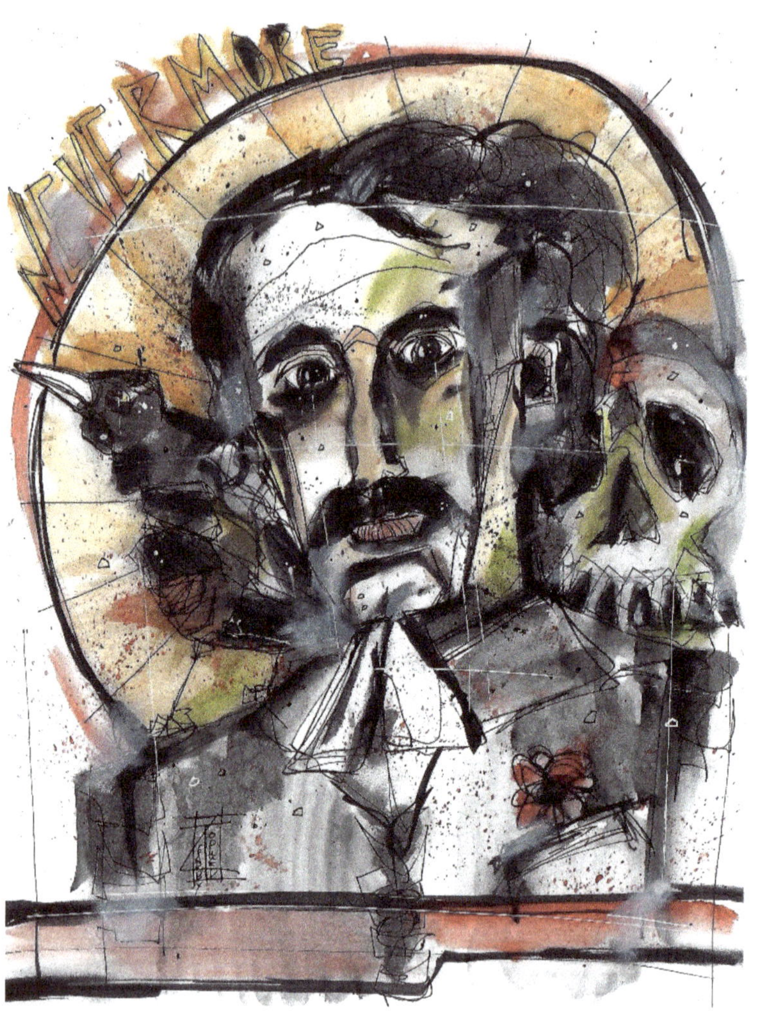
NEVERMORE

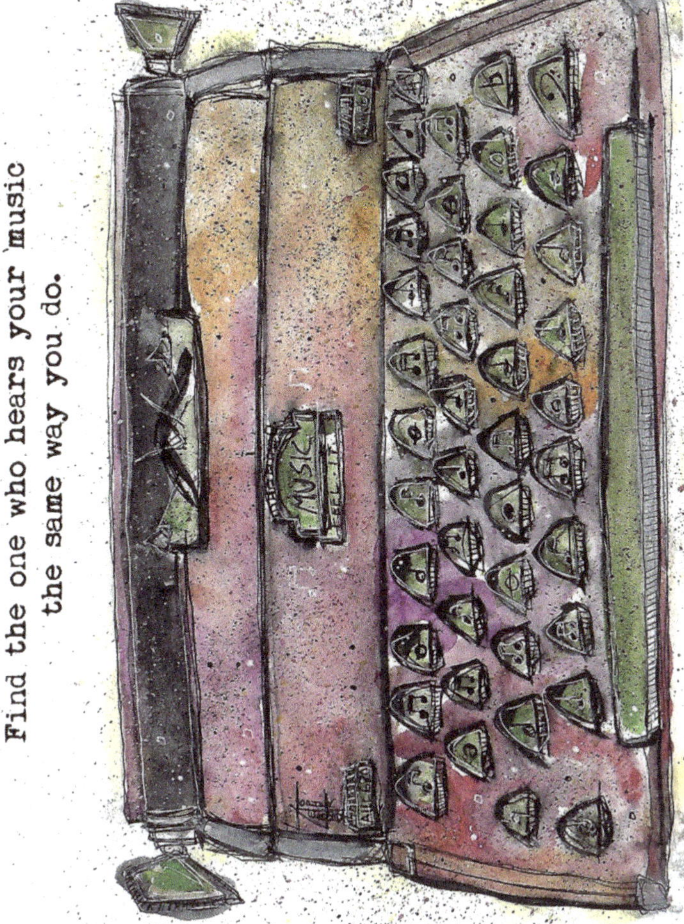
Find the one who hears your music
the same way you do.
MUSIC

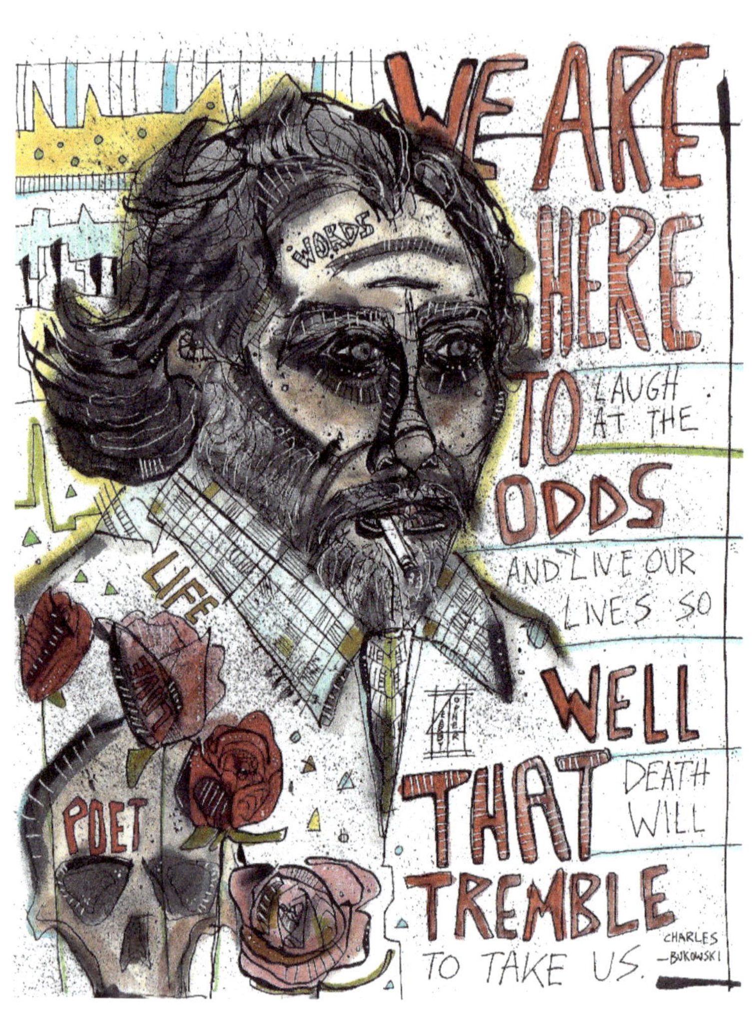
WE ARE
HERE
TO LAUGH AT THE
ODDS
AND LIVE OUR
LIVES SO
WELL
THAT DEATH WILL
TREMBLE
TO TAKE US.
CHARLES
-BUKOWSKI
WORDS
LIFE
LOVE
POET

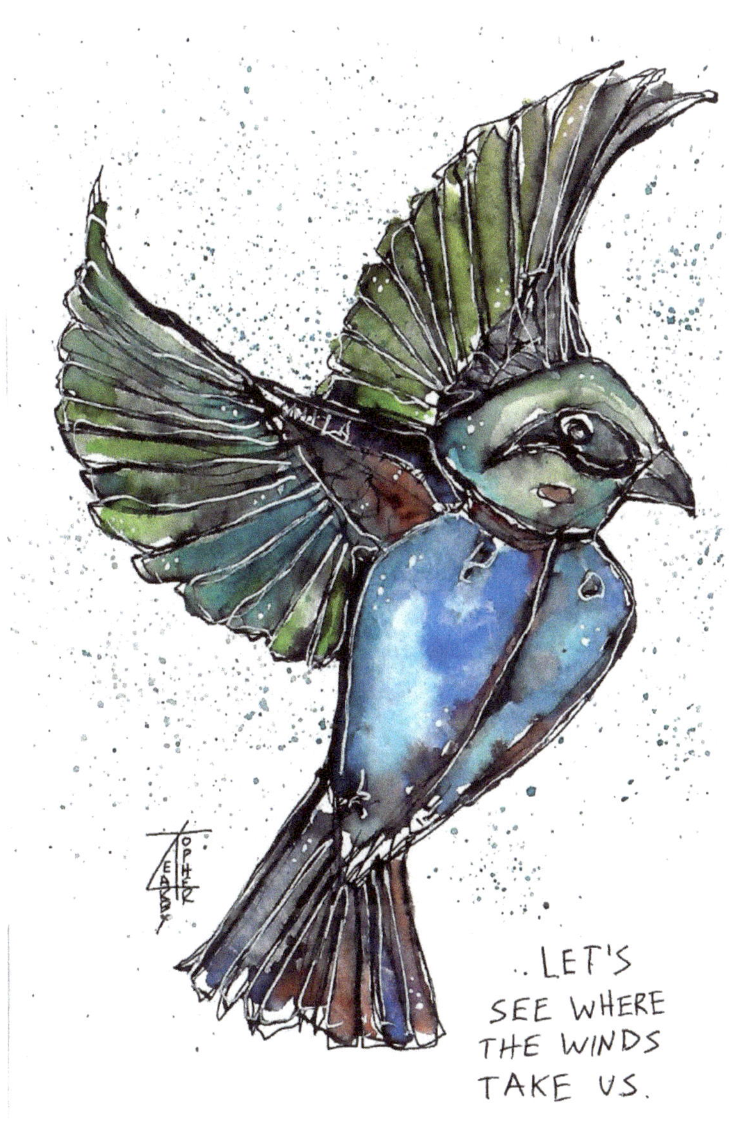
..LET'S
SEE WHERE
THE WINDS
TAKE US.

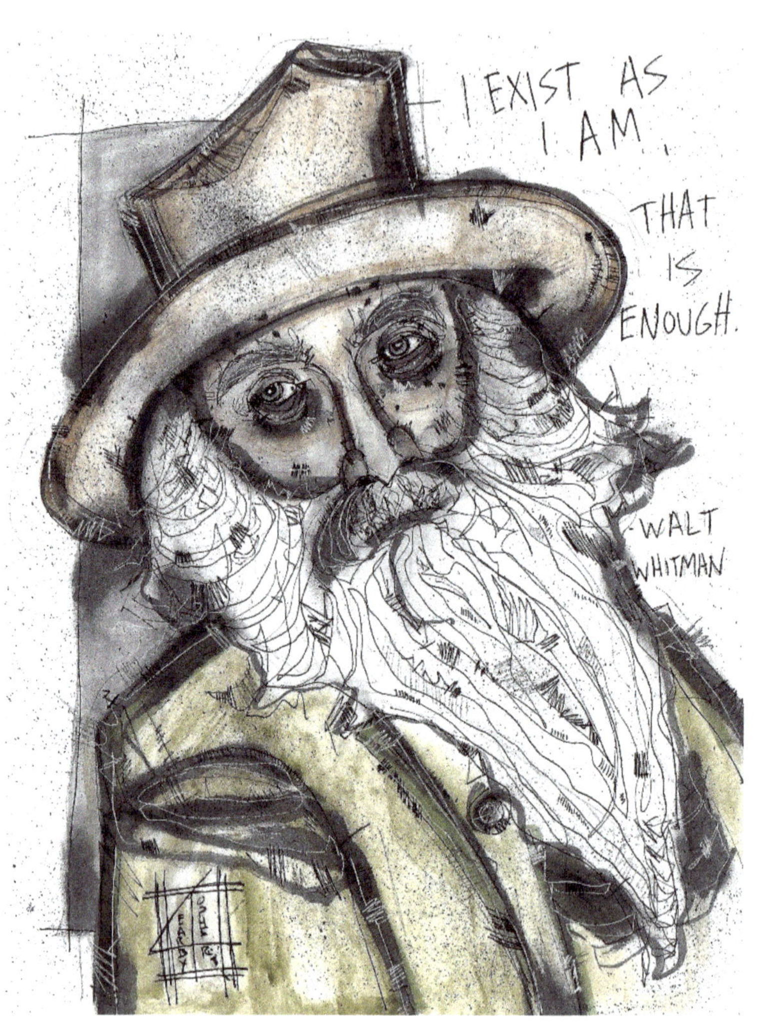
I EXIST AS
I AM,
THAT
IS
ENOUGH.
-WALT
WHITMAN

Part Three:

Journal Style Ramblings

Words are dangerous things to keep locked up; they end up turning into monsters.

Adventure

Life needs more adventure.

-

I think that's a saying on T-shirts and coffee mugs around the world. The term "adventure" has lost some of its power. Especially now in a world filled with travel bloggers and lifestyle advocates, we see travel as a way to be fiscally taken care of instead of a manner in which to feed our souls. It's all about perspective.

-

I decided a while back that I would work really hard, save money when I could, and see more of this country and this world. It's a sacrifice on most days but the hoping, planning, and making the future happen really does feed my spirit. Maybe it will take me ten years to see somewhere I've always wanted to see, maybe it will take a weekend to travel to a closer destination; I see it all as adventure.

-

Find your purpose by seeking out adventure; the heart needs to dream about what could be.

find your purpose
by seeking out
adventure;
the heart needs
to dream about
what could be.

- topher kearby

Important

It's not that life is short, it's that life is important.

-

We all have a number of days to live and then we are done, like a construction worker checking out once the bell sounds. That's it. Our job is over and it's time to go home.

-

That's beautiful. That's terrifying. That's human.

-

Yet, it isn't the fear of losing days that should move us forward; it's the understanding that our days have value that makes everything worthwhile. We are here, you and I, living. That is the gift, not the number of days we have left. If we die tomorrow, then that is how it will be. We have no more power over death than the beaches have over the waves. The universe is in motion all around us and we are travelers.

-

Take time to explore.

-

The secret to happiness is curiosity. That's been said many times by people much smarter than me, but curiosity takes effort. Exploration of the world around you takes work, planning, and a willingness to make sacrifices. We all have the same number of hours in our days, but we don't all use them the same way. If you want adventure, then go find adventure. If you want peace, then plan to know peace.

-

We waste the value of this life when we keep putting off our hopes and dreams for a day when they will make more sense. The truth is, they will never make sense. Dreams are not supposed to make sense; they are supposed to make our lives worth living. We need to spend more time listening to our spirits, and less time listening to the negative voices in our lives. Only then do we begin to realize that anything can be a reality if we put our minds and actions toward that goal.

-

I'm just a guy from Indiana trying to figure life out. I don't know any magic truths that anyone else hasn't already thought up. The only difference is I'm choosing to live my truth.

-

"Where do you see yourself in five years?"

Wanting less and living more.

it's not that life
is short,
it's that life is
important.

\- topher kearby

ART

Writing can be torture for me at times, even though it gives me life, but making art is always a joy. That's why I started scribbling, and I mean "scribbling". I couldn't draw much of anything. I seriously sucked. Mostly because I never had the guts to try.

-

That changed a few years ago.

-

Life led me to a few friends who helped guide me toward a new path. I picked up a pencil, a pen, some paints, and the rest has been a nonstop obsession. I think you need to be a little nuts to learn something new that requires so much time, but with art the process is always rewarding. I can physically see growth. This act of "doing the thing" pulled me out of a pretty bad place. I set new goals. I learned new skills. And through this pursuit I stepped out of some pretty deep darkness.

-

Read my book *People You May Know* if you want a more detailed look at my journey.

-

I am nowhere near the artist I want to be, yet I am so much further down the path than where I began.

That's the secret. Know that starting something new is a long journey; it takes a lifetime. So, it's better to be obsessed with the process rather than the result.

-

Results are only one part of the story; a very small part.

-

Making art truly makes me whole.

making art
truly
makes me
whole.

- topher kearby

Authenticity

Being consumed so often by so many isn't good for everyone. I'd wager to say it isn't good for anyone, but I don't tell people what to do. What works for you, works for you; what doesn't, doesn't. That's good. Life can be difficult and if something makes your days brighter then absorb that light.

-

It's time for a change.

-

The trees outside my apartment, the ones that I can see from my patio door, are blooming with new color. I think that's me currently. I'd say it's all of us, but again who I am to say anything about anyone but myself? Maybe ideas are like the changing, falling leaves, and maybe people who love us can see the new color in our eyes. I hope so. That's romantic as hell.

-

At my core, I am a storyteller. It has always been there, this knowledge, but it needed to be dug out from my guts again. It's an act I've done before, but this time I used a spoon…so it would hurt more (you real nerds get the reference).

-

I have been working through ideas about creativity, creation, consumption. I think many of us have figured out how to write, paint, make, post, and grow an audience, but do any of us know why? Some do, of course. Maybe everyone else besides me has it figured out and balanced like a fine-tuned pocket watch. I do not; I'm working on it.

-

This morning was soft and beautiful while Leonard Cohen's words spoke loudly. So many of his ideas in *Book of Longing* throb with palpable importance. I constantly read them over and over again as if hoping they will finally stick to my brain and not just spill out my ears while I sleep.

-

He was a true artist. I am working out what that means for me.

-

Searching for authenticity.

being consumed
so often
by so many
isn't good
for everyone.

- topher kearby

Clarity

If you have someone in your life that takes a towel and wipes away the fog of life from your eyes, that is a very rare good thing. That's why the missing starts long before they have gone.

-

Some people bring clarity.

-

I am becoming addicted to clarity. I am already longing for more of it.

dreams are not
supposed to
make sense;
they are supposed
to make our lives
worth living.

- topher kearby

Long Way

I sit at my table and reflect on a good long day.

-

I'd be lying if I said I didn't feel as if I'm going through something intense currently. I feel thunder ripple through my bones and I taste lightning on my tongue. There is no storm, but I look toward the horizon and wonder what's headed my way.

-

"Am I ready?"

-

That's life. We work and we prepare, but we are not in control. That can be a problem for someone who likes to be in control of things; that can be a problem for someone like me. It can also be incredibly thrilling. I think if I dug around in my heart and mind long enough I'd find a portion of me that wakes up only when challenges show up. I like that feeling; it's intoxicating.

-

This evening I took a long walk through the woods. I breathed in the scent of wet leaves, watched eagles soar across the river, and listened to the sounds of woodpeckers playing their wooden drums. Nature is magic. There is nothing as powerful as connecting with the soul of our world.

-

Nature teaches what words cannot.

-

I caught myself choking back tears more than once as I walked down a trail littered with rainy stones. I am not exactly sure why I ended up where I did tonight, but I somehow knew I would. Life is funny like that; we are connected to everything in ways we will never fully understand. It rained all morning, and then stopped in time for me to have time with the forest. I had no control over the passing weather, but I kept my ears open to the voice of my heart.

-

I have no answers. I am not a psychiatrist or a guru. Yet, I am aware of who I've been, who I am now, and who I might become. That is where true power rests, in the ability to own our own lives. When we place others' expectations on ourselves we also place their disappointments on our shoulders. If we fail at the goals they have set for us then we fail those people; this cycle destroys our courage.

-

Instead, plot your own course and set your own goals. If you fail then it's just part of your process and your unique journey. In this way you are no longer letting people down; you are picking yourself back up and becoming stronger each time.

-

Take the long way home. You'll be surprised how much you learn about yourself.

take the long
way home.

you'll be surprised
how much you learn
about yourself.

- topher kearby

Freedom

I'm on a mission to understand myself more completely. Recently, I've been reading, thinking, and processing more than I have in a very long time. Something inside me has awoken from a long soggy sleep, and I wonder what that means for my life moving forward.

-

"What is fulfillment?"

"What is purpose?"

-

These are questions that won't leave my mind, not that I'm kicking them out. I fall asleep thinking about these ideas, and when I wake they are there to greet me. I guess I'm either tortured or blessed with a mind that gets hungry for hearty truths. I'm not content with just accepting things at face value, I need to understand the "why" behind ideas and actions.

-

I am forever curious.

-

Today I woke with the idea of freedom on my mind. I say "idea" because what does freedom really mean? What does it look like, sound like, feel like? How does freedom relate to a purposeful life? I'm not sure, but I know it's more than an emotion; it's a way of living.

-

"Are you saying to abandon all responsibilities and just run off into the wilderness?"

-

No, not at all. There are people in our lives that are true lights. When we are around them they shine on us and we feel more like ourselves than we ever have before. That's an amazing gift. We need others. Life isn't meant to be lived completely on our own, even if it might feel easier at times. I get it. That's how it works for me as well.

-

One minute I want to build a cabin in the middle of nowhere and talk to no one, and the next minute I'm missing the people I love in a powerful way.

-

It's about balance.

-

So, what is freedom? Perhaps it is a willingness to listen to where our hearts want to travel and the belief that life can be whatever we make it.

-

No, we do not need wings to fly; we need courage.

no,
we don't need
wings to fly;
we need
courage.

- topher kearby

Daughter

The coffee is hot and my heart is open.

-

I woke this morning with so many questions on my mind. That's pretty normal, but today I couldn't get them sorted out. One question led to the next, then to the next, and then to the next. Finally, I had enough and went to the kitchen to fix some eggs.

-

Eggs in a skillet have a way of clearing my head; coffee helps too.

-

I'm thinking back to yesterday; it was a good day. I spent time in the woods and took my oldest daughter out on a date. She's growing up so fast and the thought of that is a dagger in my heart. I've been sending her pictures the last couple of weeks from when she was little. She laughs at how cute she was and I tell her she's beautiful, because she is.

-

We were shopping and she was looking at some clothes; she didn't want to buy any because she "didn't need any", and I thought that was a pretty good way to think. We joked for a minute or two about how different our fashion styles are. She said she's glittery and new and I'm an old country farm. That's about right. She's got a way with words. We laughed until she interrupted. "We are lot alike though," she said. "Our personalities. The way we see things."

-

Can't lie. That hit me in a pretty powerful way. We had been laughing, smiling, and talking about whatever was on our minds all night. As a divorced dad you worry that you might lose touch with your babies. It's an honest fear of mine, swimming its way into my blood more often than not. They have a good mom and they are good girls living a good life. I try my best to show them that I love them and that I want the best for them, but as a parent you're never sure if it's enough.

-

I put my arms around her and gave her a big hug. The kind of hug that only a dad can give his daughter. "We are a lot alike," I said. If she was paying attention she probably heard my voice catch in my throat. "I want you to know that if you ever need anything I'll be right there."

-

"I know, Daddy. I never worry."

-

That's what's bringing me to tears at my table this morning.

-

This life. How beautiful, how short, how perfect.

the coffee
is hot
and my heart
is open.

- topher kearby

Something

I took a walk today, as I tend to do, and I thought about the idea of creating art.

-

I painted a bit before I left for the day and that process always feels so honest. It's just a brush, some paint, and a blank canvas. There is nothing before I start and then there is something once I finish. That's rewarding, difficult, everything.

we give life
to art,
and art gives life
to us.

- topher kearby

Sword

Art is the sword at my side when life's beasts are waiting at the door.

-

I feel as if creating art is a way to fight off the negative energy that life brings our way. A pen and paint can't tackle all our worries, but it can help make days a bit brighter. I think that's why I have so much original art up in my apartment and why I keep getting new tattoos.

-

When I am surrounded by art I feel protected.

find your adventure,
live your dream,
for life is too
important to settle
for "good enough."

- topher kearby

Forest Fire

I sat out on my balcony for a long while tonight, thinking.

-

The air was changing here in Indiana; winter was making itself known. It was too cold to sit out there for as long as I did, but for some reason I didn't mind. The cold air made my brain feel more awake and I needed my brain to feel more awake tonight. I had a headache full of thoughts that I needed to process, and for the life of me I wasn't sure if I could pry them loose. Then, the night air set me free.

-

I was thinking about my hikes over the last couple of weeks; I was longing to be out on one again tonight, but that was impossible. Night had set in hours ago and my girls were fast asleep inside.

-

There is this thing my brain does when I'm in a busy parking lot where it kind of overloads. I'm backing my Jeep up and all of a sudden, I can see every brake light, hear every tire rub against the asphalt, and sense each person walking toward their car; it's overwhelming. I often have to take a second to gather myself before I back up the rest of the way.

-

It's a nothing moment, but enough of those moments happen over a lifetime and you realize you're just made a little differently than most people. Sometimes it's as if every sense in my body is turned up way past eleven and the switch to turn it all back down just misfires for a while. It's okay. I'm used to it by now, but my brain has kind of been stuck in that mode all day.

-

"My brain is a forest fire."

-

It's a painful kind of beauty when your emotions sit raw and exposed on top of your skin. When that happens, and it's happening a lot lately, I feel so exposed. As if the world can walk by and know everything about me—my worries, my hopes, my failures, my joys. I'm tempted to just shut it down and move on to something else, but I made a promise that I'd be true to myself. Even if that means feeling uncomfortable in my own skin for a while.

-

As the cold shook my body, I thought about the good things that were going on in my life, and I dreamed a little bit about the future. I pictured that little farm house and those few acres of land that I'm working toward, and I made a promise to myself to not give up. No one wakes up and makes things happen for you in this life; you have to make plans and go after them with your whole damn heart.

-

Nurturing your dreams is so important.
Especially after long days of putting fires out in your mind.

nurturing your
dreams is so
important.

especially after
long days of
putting fires out
in your mind.

- topher kearby

Nature

I took a hike tonight after work. It's a bit of a drive to one of the state parks I frequent, but it's always worth it. That's the thing about happiness and personal fulfillment—it takes intentional actions. It wasn't the easiest choice for me to go into the woods tonight, but I was craving the smell of the leaves and the sound of the wind moving through the trees; I listened and I found peace.

-

Life will do its best to mute your voice. Our world is built to distract us with wonderfully beautiful things that make life amazing, but they don't all feed your soul. It's become cliché to speak about "unplugging" and stepping into the wild, but there is just so much damn truth to that idea. We need less than we think we need to be happy. I'm proving that concept to myself more and more each day.

-

I am focusing on what really matters in life and putting everything else in its proper place.

-

I got off the main trail I was hiking tonight and found one that made its way through a creek bed. It was piled with boulders and slathered with mud. I had to think about every step and consider each hand placement. I laughed out loud at the sheer fun of it, like a child swinging from the branch of a tree. It was physical. It was difficult. It was gorgeous. It was everything that life is meant to be.

-

My time with the autumn woods is coming to a close. Winter's snows will be here before I know it and the landscape will change dramatically. I plan to still explore during the winter months, but I realize it will be far more difficult. So, I am taking advantage while I can; I'm storing bright memories to help me through darker times. The gray days of December will hang over me like a wet blanket for a time, and I am doing my best to prepare for that.

-

I sat and watched the sunset from the front of my Jeep as I drank iced tea from my favorite mug. I knew I had to get back home but I couldn't break myself away from that spot. I stayed, I thought, I dreamed, and I was thankful.

-

The good stuff in life is not just given away, it must be found.

the good stuff
in life
is not just
given away,
it must be
found.

- topher kearby

Finish Lines

I don't believe in finish lines.

-

I set goals in life that are difficult. I don't do this because I need to achieve a certain amount before I pass on; I set these kinds of goals because the pursuit gives me purpose. If I stop and think about how small my humanity is in comparison with the infinite universe that surrounds me, I can begin to feel unnecessary. Not unneeded or unwanted, just a bit lost.

-

That's okay. Being lost is a fine place to be.

-

I get beaten down, worn out, and defeated at least once a day. I'm joking a little bit while being absolutely serious at the same time. Life is joy, love, peace, happiness, but mostly, life is struggle. That struggle toward something gives us inner peace. Humans are wired that way. That sounds wrong, I get it, but only through accepting that life is work can we find true joy in the process of living.

-

Every perfect smile on social media and at the water cooler has a "real life" hiding just behind those pearly whites. Things are often complicated before we roll out of bed in the morning. That's normal. Having things go wrong is normal. That's a good thing for us all to remember. Life looks flawless through filtered lenses, but real life is awesomely beautiful if you dig a little deeper. The digging takes effort.

-

If you find yourself feeling like the days are getting harder and life is doing its best to kick you in the teeth, then you just might be following your dreams. That's the real truth. If you are working toward something good then it will be difficult; it should be difficult. That's how you know it's worth your hours, days, and years. The higher calling in this life is to dream so big that it might take two lifetimes to get halfway to where you want to go.

-

"It's not impossible, it just feels that way because it's worth the effort."

if you find yourself
feeling like the days
are getting harder and
life is doing its best
to kick you in the teeth,
then you just might be
following your dreams.

- topher kearby

Muse

When I have questions I often turn to Johnny Cash for answers.

-

This weekend has already had its share of challenges. That's life; the good comes with the bad. I'm not complaining. Today was a hell of a good day. I spent it with some of my favorite people: my girls and Johnny Cash.

-

It might be a bit of a strange relationship I have with the late singer, but it's been one of my longest. His music has always spoken loudly to me, and his life has been a source of constant curiosity. He was conflicted, damaged, compassionate, loving, passionate, and talented beyond compare; he was powerfully human. I'd call him my muse if that wouldn't dilute his legacy.

-

I relate to the parts of him that shattered as much as I connect with the pieces of him that soared. His music is as much about speaking as it is playing, and I feel that's the way I try to write. I want to have a conversation with people. I feel Cash probably felt the same.

-

I'm no good in a crowd, I get uncomfortable and look for the closest exit; but give me a one on one or a small group of close friends and I'll open up my story book. I crave intimacy and run from formality. That's why I talk about the soul so much and why I never talk about wanting to fit in. I care more about the deep-down bits of the human condition—the good stuff. That's why when I have a quiet Saturday afternoon, like I did today, I put on Cash and let his music examine my heart.

-

"Love is like that perfect song on the radio. When it's in your heart you lose all track of time."

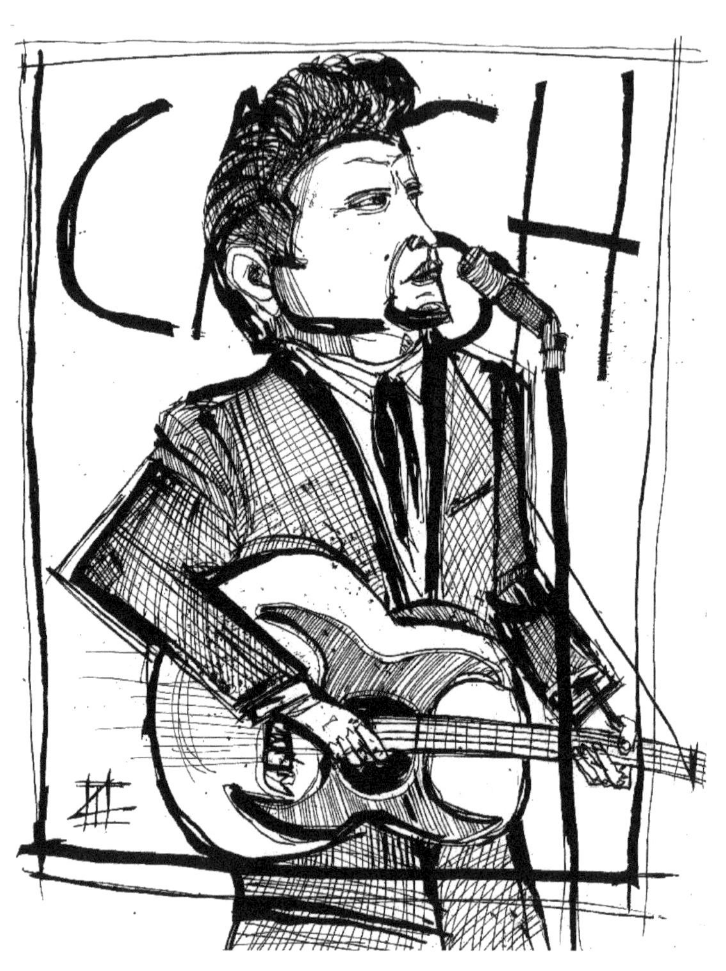

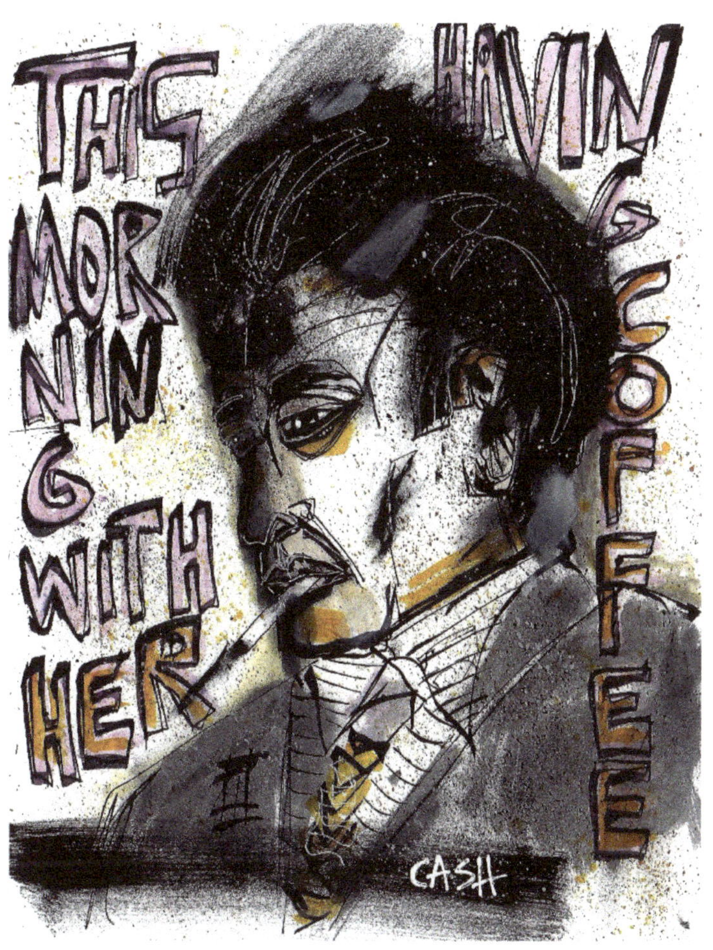
THIS MOR NIN G WITH HER
HAVIN G COFFEE
CASH

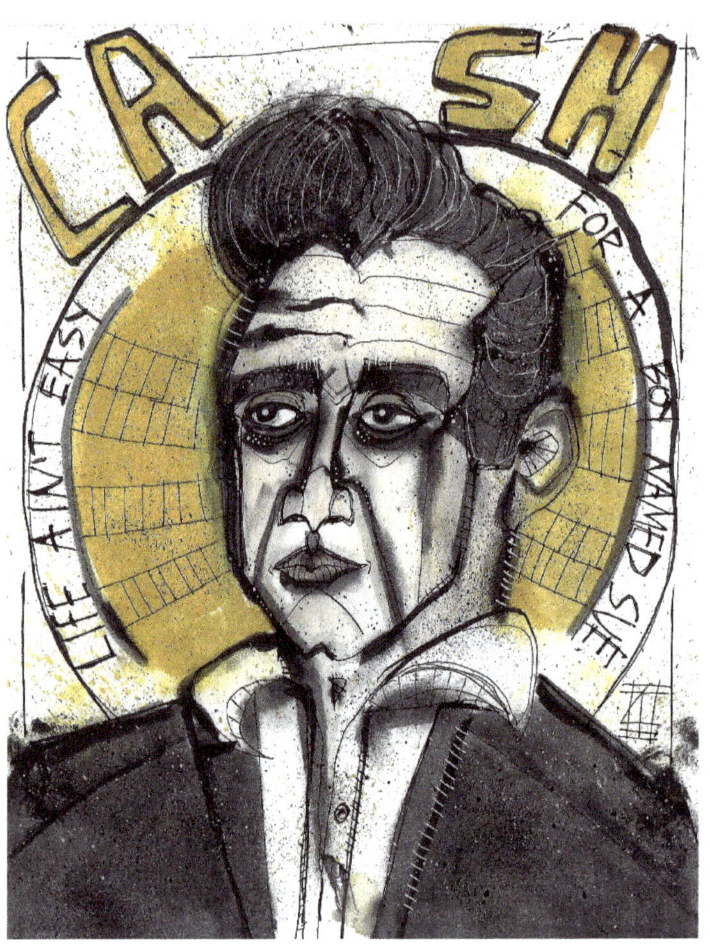
CASH
LIFE AIN'T EASY FOR A BOY NAMED SUE

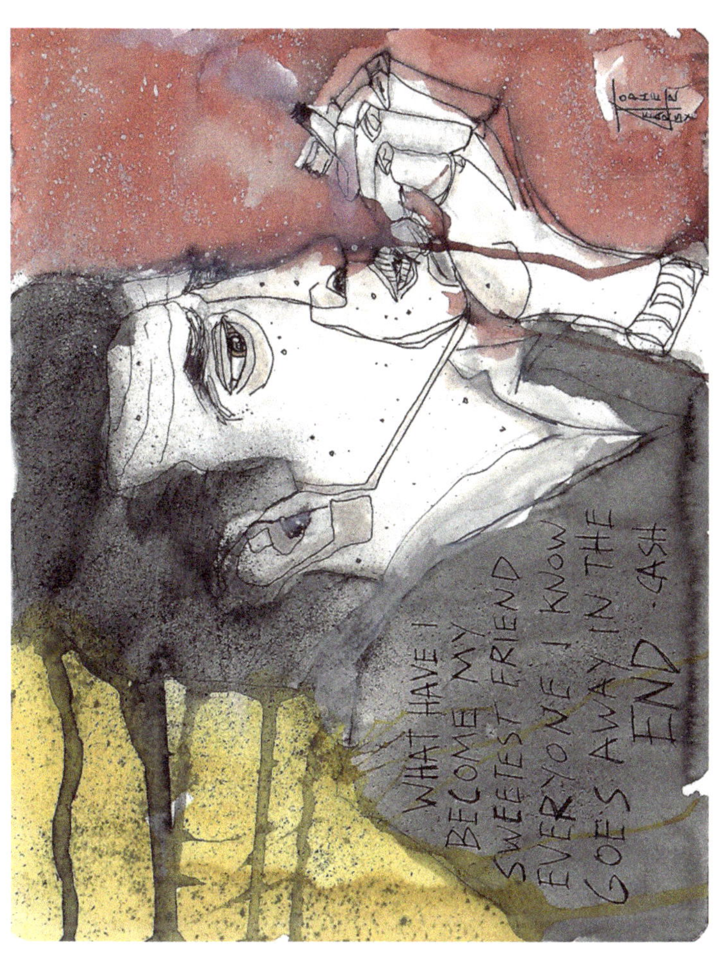
WHAT HAVE I
BECOME MY
SWEETEST FRIEND
EVERYONE I KNOW
GOES AWAY IN THE
END
-CASH

Escape

I get tired from being locked up in a building all day.

-

I left work this afternoon feeling like my head might explode. It didn't make a lot of sense, because I truly enjoy my job and it was a pretty good day. Yet, still I was completely drained by the time I sat down in my Jeep to drive home. I couldn't pin down what my issue was, but then through a good conversation I realized I was wiped out from fighting the "box" all day.

-

"I am always plotting my escape."

-

Not everyone is wired the same, that's not a newsflash, but it does take effort to remember that idea. Your happiness is not my happiness, and your purpose isn't necessarily my purpose. That's good. What motivates me and wakes me up in the morning might cause you a panic attack; what puts you to sleep peacefully at night may wake me up on the wrong side of the bed. We need to stop trying to emulate others' happiness and discover what our personal purpose really looks like.

-

My happiness looks a lot like a dirt covered trail in the woods.

-

I find a lot of peace amongst the trees. I can't fully explain it, but it's like I can finally breathe when my boots hit the ground. Concrete walls and glass windows are great to keep us safe and warm, but the human spirit needs a relationship with the wilderness. Our fingers need to feel the dirt, our ears need to hear the birds, and our lips need to kiss the wind. Without this intimate relationship with Mother Nature we lose a special part of our humanity.

-

It's time to remind you that I'm not an expert on anything. I don't have a psychology degree that gives me credibility when I say, "Go hug a tree. You'll be happier." But I personally believe that you would be a little happier if you threw your arms around a big oak. You may look a little silly to the couple jogging past you, but they look a little silly in their matching five-hundred-dollar jogging outfits. We all look a little silly. Who gives a shit at the end of the day? Just go do what makes you happy.

-

The autumn leaves have fallen now, but the winter is waking up a new kind of beautiful all around me.

we need to stop
trying to emulate
others' happiness
and discover what
our personal purpose
really looks like.

- topher kearby

Self-Aware

I move slowly.

-

It takes a long while to get to know me. I'm easy to meet and I would like to think of myself as kind, but I don't consider myself "easy to know". Maybe that's how we all are, but I only know myself. I do understand that I am guarded in areas where some people are far more open. I'm not sure why, probably genetics, but I hold the truest parts of myself way below the surface.

-

I truly know me, and that's enough.

-

Even after years of having certain people in my life I still feel very vulnerable opening all the way up. It's uncomfortable to rip out my heart and hand it to another human, while trusting they won't just toss it in the garbage. That's happened before and maybe that's why now I'm more careful.

-

I also take a long time to feel. I'm learning this about myself. Emotions don't register with me right away like they do with other people; my emotions take longer to surface. It might be hours or even days, but eventually it will all hit me and I'll feel everything. My processing takes time, and life doesn't always give me that time. So, I get messed up a lot with my feelings. Maybe someone in my life has moved past where I am with an issue, and I'm still miles behind. That can make a person feel very misunderstood.

-

Life is a lot of feeling misunderstood.

-

Thankfully, I'm at the point in my life where I am confident with who I am and where I am going. Even if I seem lost most of the time. My brain misfires some days, my heart often drowns with intense passions, and my feet are always ready to find a new path to explore. How I live my life may look strange to some people and that's just fine with me. I'm a proud weirdo and I know that will never change.

-

"Happiness is being weird enough that most people leave you alone, and the ones who stay truly love you."

happiness is being
weird enough
that most people
leave you alone,
and the ones who stay
truly love you.

- topher kearby

Weird

I like being weird.

-

One of my more popular sayings has to do with falling in love with a weird one. I've always treasured the idea that people identify with that quote. Being weird is this uniquely human concept that when embraced can really allow us to live more freely.

-

Weird isn't something to be ashamed of; weird is a way of life.

-

I channel a lot of emotions into my art, especially when I'm not able to put them into words. Art has guided me through some major emotional moments in my life and most days I'd be lost without that kind of self-expression.

-

Life is better with a weird one; life is better when we love our true selves.

fall in love with
a weird one,
someone not quite
right in the head.

life is far more
interesting when
love is odd.

- topher kearby

Worry

"What now?"

"What next?"

-

I'd be lying if I said I had a completely thought out plan for my future. I'm not lost, as the saying goes, but I haven't completely found my place in the world. Yes, I'm happy with where I am now in life but that doesn't mean I'll be happy on this path forever. I'm built to change; I transform often. My soul is wired to improvise.

-

The sun was out in full force today during my hike and I couldn't have been more thankful. Indiana gets pretty gray this time of year, so to get a full day with such bright celestial energy was incredible. The trails I took this afternoon surprised me with their difficulty; it was exciting. I had to really think about how to approach certain parts of the path and I could feel my brain smiling. That sounds silly, but I swear it's true. We humans are designed to overcome difficult situations; challenges feel good.

-

That's why I don't stress too much about not having a perfect design for my future. If someone asked me for a five or ten-year plan I'd say, "I'll figure it out." And I will figure it out. That doesn't mean I don't spend nights dreaming, thinking, and making choices toward a purposeful life. It does mean that I'm willing to let the world come at me and I'll adjust and improvise.

-

I can't let fear win.

-

Worry doesn't give me anything for the time I spend with it; it's not a good investment. Tomorrow will still come, hopefully, and bring with it whatever it has in store. I have to let go of not being in control of everything and by doing so I'll set my spirit free to grow.

-

I still stumble with this pursuit all the time, but I'm getting better. I'm learning to celebrate the small victories. They add up over a lifetime.

worry doesn't give
me anything for
the time i spend
with it;
it's not a good
investment.

- topher kearby

Pragmatic Empath

I think and I plan. I make goals and I set my mind on the future. I read and I listen. I wonder and I consider all my options. I am pragmatic.

-

Yet, if someone with an aching heart walks by me, I feel it. I feel it so powerfully sometimes that it nearly cuts me off at the knees. I try and act like I'm not a sponge for emotions by pretending nothing really bothers me, but the truth is that everything moves me in some way. It's why I have to cut off so much at times just so I can function.

-

I want to have a plan but if the right emotions hit I will spin wildly in a new direction.

-

That can be a difficult way to live.

-

I realize this isn't an unusual way of living, but it's my way of living. That's why I write the way I write about what I write about. This is my journey toward the end and the story of the things I think about along the way. One step at a time until I take my final step (hopefully a very long time from now).

-

The truth is no one knows if the last moment will be now or one hundred years from now. That's beautiful; if I could know, I wouldn't want to. That would ruin the adventure of it all.

-

So, what are we to do when at our core we see the world as a place that needs to make sense but we are constantly overwhelmed by emotions? Good question. I don't have an answer. I do know that I believe it is practical to feel the earth's heartbeat as we walk in unison with the universe. That also means having a heightened sense of connection with other people. When someone hurts, we feel it. When someone is angry, we feel it. When someone is full of love, we feel it.

-

It's a gift; it's a burden.

It's called being a pragmatic empath.

i am a
pragmatic
empath.

- topher kearby

Human Stuff

Ask me what I did right yesterday and I'll mumble around for a few minutes without really saying anything. Ask me what I did wrong yesterday and I'll deliver a thirty-minute soliloquy detailing everything that I messed up with precise description.

-

I am made of human stuff; that stuff is complicated.

-

I'm not sure why most of us are wired this way but I feel like it's a common way to process a day. We get stuck on the bad and rarely spend much time on the good. Maybe it's how we evolved as humans, because if we spent too much time celebrating a successful hunt then we would let our guard down and get eaten by a saber-toothed cat. I'm not certain but that kind of makes sense.

-

The world today isn't like it once was but that doesn't mean life is easy. I still feel that if I let my guard down too much then something (or someone) will "eat" me. That's silly, I get it, but it's a real feeling.

-

If I spend too much time basking in the sun then I won't be able to survive when the cold hits. I think about that a lot. I'm thinking about that today.

-

I'm wondering if I'm ready.

i am made of
human stuff;
that stuff is
complicated.

- topher kearby

Intentional

My brain gets caught on ideas and has to work them out before it lets them go.

-

Recently, I've been spending a lot of time in silence. I might be walking, sitting, or driving but I'm not saying much of anything. Maybe a mumble or a blurt of emotion here or there, but mostly my words are still. This has been a conscious choice. I wanted to force myself to spend time with myself. That sounds a bit strange because we are always with ourselves, yet taking time to truly visit with yourself takes an intentional act. It takes making hard choices.

-

Intentional acts will change your life.

-

I always told myself that if I lived near the mountains I would be happier because the mountains would always be there and I could hike them anytime I wanted. It was a dream; it was also an excuse. I am good at disguising excuses with ideals.

-

"If I was in the best place doing the best things I would be the best version of myself."

-

It was time to call bullshit. Happiness isn't dependent on location. Even if I uprooted my life and moved to the most beautiful place on earth I would still bring my problems with me. Once I realized this fact I began to dig into my spiritual guts. It's a messy business. It takes time and persistence.

-

Happiness takes effort.

-

I'm not a life expert. I don't know what I'm doing and I rarely know what I'm talking about. I make more mistakes before breakfast than some people make their whole lives. That being said, I know some actions have helped me grow a little bit recently. I've become aware of what I'm putting into my mind and body. This means different things for different people, but for me it means staying curiously conscious about what I consume. That's a tongue twister.

-

It's cliché at this point to say that winter is coming, but that's the truth. Gray skies and cold winds are blowing in and I am doing my best to prepare. I want to build up my spirit enough for it not to hammer me too hard this year. That's the "why" behind what I'm doing; it's time to figure out the "how".

-

When we take time to get to know ourselves we find out who the hell we really are.

when we take time to
get to know ourselves
we find out who the hell
we really are.

- topher kearby

Fight

Some mornings I wake up ready for a fight.

-

I'm a pretty laid-back guy, I don't let things get me too off track too often. Yet, there is one person that I always seem to be at odds with; I like to fight myself. This morning I want to hit life so hard that it hits me back. That sounds strange, but I'm realizing that's just how I am.

-

I don't like "easy" things and I get real weird real fast when I start to feel settled. My skin starts to crawl and my eyes start twitching and every ounce of my being becomes uncomfortable. When this happens, I've been known to shrug it off and just compartmentalize. I don't want to do that this time. I don't want to forget.

-

I'm walking headstrong into the waves of the crashing storm, fully aware that the power of this world might wreck me.

-

My mind needs to be bright and alert. I want to think about thoughts that I have been too scared, too lazy, or too ill-equipped to think about before. I started my day with tears again, which isn't normal for me. I was tempted to shove certain painful truths out of my head and move on with my day; instead I let them stay. It's uncomfortable to have all these unwanted guests in my head, but I know that I need to speak with them so I can learn why they are here and what they need to say.

-

I can see that "good-good" life peeking its head out just over the horizon, and I can also see everything that stands in my way. I'm readying myself, I'm preparing my mind, and I am not ignoring my pain.

-

If I don't have my back against the wall working toward something new I get lost pretty quickly. That's why it's healthy for me to set big unbelievable goals, and it's why I push myself to try new experiences. I have no real interest in success, but I have a very real interest in understanding this life that I'm living. I think to do that I need to struggle with myself; it's how I grow.

-

Maybe you are like me and maybe you are the complete opposite; the truth is whatever works for you is what works. It's time to dig a little deeper into who we are and how we tick, so we can work through some of our pain and live a more fulfilled future.

-

Keep working. Keep fighting. The best is yet to come.

i can see that
"good-good" life peeking
its head out just over
the horizon, and i can
also see everything that
stands in my way.

- topher kearby

Sledgehammer

Some allow others in with ease; to know me you need a sledgehammer.

-

I'm typically a guarded person. I protect my true self as a mother bear protects her cubs—with teeth and claws. That changes if I trust you; if I trust you then I love you.

-

It's a simple system that works well for me in life. I'm not a "tribe" type of person. I'm more of a loner who has a few special people in his life. I like it that way. I keep my circle small and my heart big for those people. I feel as though if anyone that I love ever needed me, then I'd be there in a heartbeat. I trust that they would do the same, because they *have* done the same.

-

Maybe you're a little like me too. You love quickly but develop relationships slowly. Friendships and relationships are earned over time, not given away like candy at a parade. Honestly, the years have placed heavy stones around my heart that take effort to move or knock down. If you are willing to stay with me and work through the rubble, then you and I will be close. I'll do the same with you if you let me. That's how love works.

-

We should tell people in our lives that we love them more often. We should walk right up to them, wrap our arms around them, and say, "I love you and you matter to me." Hugs aren't for everyone, but for me they are everything. I get that from my mother. I'm a hugger. You just have to deal with that if we're friends.

-

So, I guess it looks like I'm complicated. I'm distant, but long to be close. I'm guarded, but once I let you in it's forever.

-

Being alone is a good thing, but so is spending time in the embrace of someone who loves you.

we should tell people
in our lives that we
love them more often.
we should walk right
up to them, wrap our
arms around them, and
say,
"i love you and you
matter to me."

- topher kearby

Dawn

I'm thankful for the mornings.

-

I often write about the dawn of a new day, because it is such a gift. The night can carry with it all sorts of menace, but when that sun rises out of the sky I feel renewed; every day I am born again.

-

I was hurrying around this morning getting my girls off to school. I fixed some eggs, gave some big hugs, and drove my Jeep an hour to work. It's a long daily drip but I really don't mind. It gives me time to drink a big cup of black coffee, think about the day ahead, and watch the sun color the sky. I can't complain about a life that good.

-

I do believe that we are made in the fires of life. Who we really are becomes known when we are tested. When life gets impossible, we find a way to make it possible. I love that idea; I believe it with my whole heart. Yet, every day isn't a trial nor is every victory solely found after fighting off problems. Some things in life are just good, and I'm trying to recognize that more often.

-

This new day is good. That is a simple powerful truth.

-

We humans are this giant community of beating hearts that stretches around the world and back again; there is power in that. Yes, the world can be a place that makes us feel a lot of pain; it's also a place where we can feel so much purpose.

-

"Out of the night and into the dawn."

yes, the world can
be a place that makes
us feel a lot of pain;
it's also a place where
we can feel so much purpose.

- topher kearby

Coffee

I still smell the coffee on my grandfather's table.

-

Today, coffee is a lifestyle; there is a beautiful shop on every town corner. Yet, it wasn't like that when I was growing up, at least not where I'm from. I remember the cans of Folgers that my grandfather scooped mounds from. He was always up early, as was my grandmother. They ran a farm together and mornings always came early for those that worked the land.

-

If I shut my eyes I swear I can still smell the aroma, still see the soft morning light falling on the kitchen table, and still remember thinking that the whole scene was something special. It was; it still is.

-

Memories wake so powerfully through remembered aromas.

hot coffee
and wild hope.

some mornings
that is enough.

- topher kearby

Time

I woke up a little early today to spend time with myself.

-

I typically get up around the same time in the morning, give or take a few minutes. Last night I could feel my brain twitching a bit as I lay in bed, and I recognized what that meant—my thoughts needed to be processed.

-

Life doesn't hand us more time just because our brains get a little foggy. The days keep pushing us along no matter our needs, yet there is power in how we choose to spend our time. I made a choice to make time for myself; nothing important happens on accident.

-

I set my alarm for thirty minutes earlier than usual. It was supposed to snow a little bit last night but nothing came of it. The weather always changes. By all accounts it was a normal gray November morning in Indiana. I opened my patio door for a bit and let some of the cold air swirl through my apartment. I made my eggs, packed my lunch, slid the patio door shut, laced up my boots, and locked the door behind me. The whole time my brain was itching to just get "out".

-

"I keep getting stuck on the why of things."

-

I pulled my Jeep over on the edge of some gravel road in the middle of nowhere, rolled down my windows, and stared out at the horizon for a while. It wasn't a spectacular view, but that made it all the more important to really look. I wasn't thinking about anything in particular, yet I could feel everything being thought of at once inside my head. This human thing is a strange pursuit. We work, plan, learn, grow, fail, and repeat it all over again thousands of times (if we are lucky). Some days that cycle feels like prison. Other days it feels like purpose.

-

I think back to a time long ago when the earth was nothing like it is today. The mountains were buried beneath the soil and the seas were new. Everything was waiting to be born. That's how I feel today. I am waiting on what's next, without knowing what that is. It's painfully perfect.

-

Maybe the secret to life is understanding that the "now" is the next. Where we are is everywhere we will ever need to be, no matter where we end up.

where we are is
everywhere we will
ever need to be,
no matter where we
end up.

- topher kearby

Journey

The joy is the journey.

-

I took a long walk yesterday afternoon. It was cold and the sky was painted with the gray of winter. It was a beautiful time spent doing my favorite activity: thinking. Before my hike I could feel anxiety filling my chest like water filling an empty bowl, and I knew I needed to do something physical; I needed to push myself.

-

There is something about a physical challenge that settles my nerves. I think that's why I enjoy working out in the country so much when I get a chance. Nothing comes easy when you work the land, and there is a part of our humanity that longs for that experience.

-

When I started my hike there were about ten cars parked at the entrance. when I left, my Jeep was the only vehicle around. I didn't plan to be there as long as I was, but I stayed as long as I needed; some thoughts take more time to process.

-

I met a man by the water a couple of miles into my journey. He was talking to himself a little bit and it seemed kind of strange at first. Then I remembered I often talk to myself and I'm sure that seems pretty strange too. I waved to him and began to walk on by.

He called out, "I like to watch the water. It clears my head."

"I get that," I replied. "That's why I walk."

"Me too," he said.

I smiled earnestly. "Take care. Enjoy your time."

-

I don't know anything else about that man so I won't place my guesses on him, but I bet we are more alike than different. There's a part of human nature that calls out for water, trees, wind, and the sun that can't be answered with anything else. I think when we deprive ourselves of spiritual moments in the wilderness or by the sea, we rob ourselves of peace.

-

Life will not give you purpose laid out like a feast; you must seek it out (especially on the difficult days). I'm working on being intentional, I'm building better days, I'm pursuing the impossible, and I'm clearing out the excuses that I've let block my way.

i think when we deprive
ourselves of spiritual
moments in the wilderness
or by the sea, we rob
ourselves of peace.

- topher kearby

Moments

Don't skip the small moments between the big events.

-

I remember reading a story when I was young about a boy who had a magical ball of string. He would pull the string little by little and move time forward. He used it to skip "boring" and "difficult" moments to get to the "good stuff". The boy gets to the end of his life and realizes that he actually has everything that really mattered. All those slow or painful moments that he skipped were really the parts that would have given his existence purpose.

-

I am reminding myself of that story today. I get so anxious to jump to the next big thing that I can lose track of the present or become frustrated with the struggle of the "now". I sometimes feel like I am just waiting to be moved. Yet, if I look around me right now it is clear that I am already in motion. That movement is the essence of life. Recognizing that gives meaning to lost moments.

-

I remember the tough parts of my life—the struggle, the hard work, the pain, the failure—far more than I remember the moments of victory. That isn't because I'm a masochist and just dwell on the pain. It is because those are the moments in which I had to fight and grow more than I ever had to before. I met a challenge head on and I walked out on the other side with a new perspective and a new set of abilities.

-

Learning to be still and appreciate the present is a learned skill. I think it's ingrained in us to always be planning and alert about the future, because we need to be ready. Yet, by solely focusing on that plan we miss out on the good stuff that happens every day. Sometimes that good stuff is difficult stuff. Sometimes we get worn about by the difficult stuff. I get it. It's all about perspective.

-

It's been said so many times in so many ways that it is not about the destination, it is about the journey. I believe that with my whole heart. My life will be spent learning to appreciate the between moments. I will learn to stop and notice life as it happens. There isn't one big finish line that I'm running toward. Purpose is simply a series of victories and failures all along the way.

-

Let's all journey together. One step at a time.

don't skip
the small moments
between the
big events.

- topher kearby

Hope

Life will take whatever you give it; today I plan to give it hope.

-

I woke up this morning with dreams in my eyes. I could see far ahead into the future and it was beautiful. I felt a life well lived. I tasted the sweat from days spent toiling in the sun. I remembered long nights where I wrestled with impossible ideas. I heard laughter. I breathed in joy. I dreamed of a wonderful life. It was difficult; it was perfect.

-

Then I woke up.

-

Dreams are a good way to move through the difficult days in life. There is magic in looking ahead at what might be and putting plans in place to make it happen. Even if those plans are difficult; especially if those plans are difficult. Life is more hardship than happiness and that doesn't mean that life is bad. I believe that life is good—really good. And it is good because of the struggle. It makes the victories so much more powerful.

-

Time passes and on the other side of the pain we see growth—real growth. Not the kind of growth you can buy at the super store down the street, but true life-altering growth. That kind of evolution only happens when we are pushed to our breaking points, and then we realize that we are so much stronger than we ever dreamed.

-

Do you remember how that feels? Shut your eyes for a moment or two and think back to a time where you overcame something huge in your life. I have heard so many stories from people recently about how they fought through seemingly impossible days. And you know what? They are changed people now. Each stronger than when they started their unique journey. Do you remember how you fought and how you survived? Celebrate that moment again today.

-

I can think back to a time in my life where I thought I couldn't move forward any longer. Life was too strong and I was too weak to keep fighting. I had given it all. I had taken too much. It seemed like there was no way out. But here I am, still standing.

-

I celebrate that today. Through that experience I found out who I really was. I wasn't weak or fragile. I was a fire waiting to be lit.

-

Even though the days ahead are heavy with challenges and uncertainty, today I hope.

-

Because life is worth it.

life will take
whatever you give it;
today i plan to
give it hope.

- topher kearby

Masks

These many masks we wear to make others comfortable with who we are end up killing us.

-

Take a walk with me. Let's look at the hundreds of trees in the forest. You can point out the differences between the many oaks and I'll talk about my favorite designs that make up the sprawling branches of the maples. Not once will we say, "I like this one because it is just like that one" or "I wish this branch was more like that branch". We don't require similarities in nature; we don't expect things to be the same in the wild. Then, why the hell do we demand that from each other?

-

We are a world of individuals that crave to be accepted.

-

I think that's why we struggle so much with identity. We feel as if we are a thousand different people to a thousand different people, and never truly anyone. That's a complicated bag of emotions, but if you feel that way you aren't alone. From birth, society places us in environments where we have to learn to fit in or be rejected. So, we learn to blend, dull, and disappear.

-

I do think it can be better; we can be happier with not being accepted.

-

Maybe it comes with age, but I'm finally happy with who I am. I've always been one to be pretty comfortable in my own shoes, even if those shoes are a bit awkward or strange, but I was also a people pleaser. I wanted to make sure that everyone was happy with me in any situation that came up. I would twist myself into a million different shapes in order to fit into whatever puzzle was being played. It was exhausting, and that lifestyle eventually took too much. Finally, I just decided to be myself. What happened next was the most powerful season of growth in my life.

-

If you know me now, then you really know me. Even if you only know me from this page. I write from my heart and I live authentically. I'm not here to tug on your heartstrings with words that I don't believe or art that I'm not proud of. I'm on a journey of self-discovery that is taking me places I've never been. I don't plan to ever fit in again.

-

I'm learning to love to walk in my own shoes.

i'm on a journey of
self-discovery that
is taking me places
i've never been.

i don't plan to ever
fit in again.

- topher kearby

Poetry

I often find myself lost in poetry, but it isn't words that keep me captivated. It is the swaying of the trees in the wind, it is the powdered snow that covers the ground each morning, it is the sun's warmth, it is the stars' light. It is everything.

-

Life is both the poet and the poetry.

-

Today I am missing my autumn lessons spent walking through the forest. I can still feel the breeze against my face and I can still see the vibrant colors that painted the sky, but my memories are beginning to fade. It was such a powerful time of transformation for me and to say I don't dream about those days would be a lie. I long for the muddy trails and the conversations with the sky. It was a season come and gone and trying to hold onto it will not bring it back.

-

It is time to move forward.

-

My boots need to hit the snow in the same way they did during the warmer months. Yet, in my heart I know it will not be the same. As humans we foolishly long for that sameness. We go to the same well hoping to be nourished as we were before, but it doesn't work like that. Life doesn't work like that. We are drawn forward by an ever-advancing and expanding universe.

-

Longing for the past will steal our futures.

-

I look to my graceful woodland teachers for guidance once more as I begin to open my heart again. The seasons have changed, and I with them, so there is no need to lament what has been lost. Ice wraps the branches of the mighty oaks and the frigid air strangles the color from the wildflowers. It looks as if all life has been stolen from the earth, yet rebirth is still happening. I can feel it.

-

There is far more to this life than what can be seen and what can be held in our hands. There is energy flowing through everything that binds all things. That's a beautiful image. That's a beautiful hope. We are all on the same journey of understanding. That's why we can learn so much from the steady nature of the trees. They are forever changing yet still resolute.

-

We long to be more than what is expected of us and desire to be more than what is seen; we long to be complete.

life is both
the poet
and the poetry.

- topher kearby

Shut Up

Life holds me by the tongue sometimes and doesn't let me speak. I try and fight it, but it's no use. I'm not as in control as I think I am, and that idea wrecks me some days. I want to have some power over what happens in life, yet I truly have power over very little. I am reminded of this fact when I am silent. That's why the universe shuts me up—so I'll actually listen.

-

Sometimes that "shut up" hurts.

-

I've been working through a lot of new ideas lately. A few of them have shown up in my writing but most have just been filling up my head like wet socks in the dryer; nothing matches, everything is spinning, and I need to change the lint filter. Needless to say, my brain gets tired of all the ideas. I think that's what I'm feeling now—tired.

-

I know that the people we think have it all figured out truly don't have it all figured out. I like writers and creators who just leave it all out for people to examine. "This is me. It's kind of shitty, but I'm doing the best I can." I respect that because I can learn from that kind of person.

I can't pull anything from a "best life" advertisement on an Instagram story.

-

So, here I am opening up my guts once again in hopes that the process moves me forward. It isn't easy but I believe in being genuine. In truth I can't figure out what's next for my journey. That's not really a major issue for anyone else but me, but for me it matters.

-

That's why my face has been a little more "scowly" than normal. This body of mine is retaining tension as if it's waiting on something. What is it waiting on? Well, that's what's bothering me.

-

I'm not good at standing still.

-

I'm happy when I'm moving. The winter slows my body down a bit, that's not a surprise, but it doesn't slow my mind down. I often get very introspective this time of year. I begin to dig deep into my core and sometimes what is revealed is difficult to understand; I am making an effort to examine the difficult stuff with curious eyes.

-

What's next?

Maybe the truth.

silence is always willing
to share its wisdom.

we just need to learn
to shut up long enough
to hear its voice.

- topher kearby

Better

Some people make us better; that's beautiful and terrifying.

-

We need people. That's not a secret. But for an independent type of personality, that can be a difficult truth to accept. It's difficult for me.

-

"Why?"

-

The "why" is a tough thought to unpack. There is a lot of pain mixed up with the need to be independent and in charge of my own destiny. I understand that now. Some of that pain was brought on by my own choices, and a bit of that pain was just life doing what it does. I'm opening up and considering all ideas these days. I want to be honest with myself in order to grow. That doesn't make the process easy.

-

The feeling of being loved beyond the level that you think you deserve is such a powerful experience. To be seen—truly seen—for more than just your mistakes. To be lifted higher than you've ever been lifted before gives you such a fresh view of what is possible. That is a gift and I am thankful to have people in my life that see me in that way. I treasure each of them, even if I'm not the best at letting them know how I feel. I need to do better at that but it's a struggle for me, being that vulnerable. I'm a work in progress.

-

"I need you."

-

Even writing that phrase makes my stomach tighten a little bit. Not because I don't believe it, but because opening up in that way isn't something I'm great at. I can pour into complete strangers and tell my friends how much I care about them, but place me in a situation where I am completely vulnerable and watch as I close myself up. It's like some kind of reverse magic trick. "Watch as I turn my insecurities into walls!"

-

Not every experience is meant to be shared but I try to focus on my struggles in hopes that anyone who reads this and feels the same will feel less alone. You're not alone. Trust me. We all have a lifetime's worth of baggage that we bring into every relationship. The unpacking of that baggage takes time and patience. Don't rush the process of healing.

-

Being vulnerable is beautiful and unnerving, but it's worth it when you find someone who truly loves you for who you are.

let's start again -
this time with our
real selves.

\- topher kearby

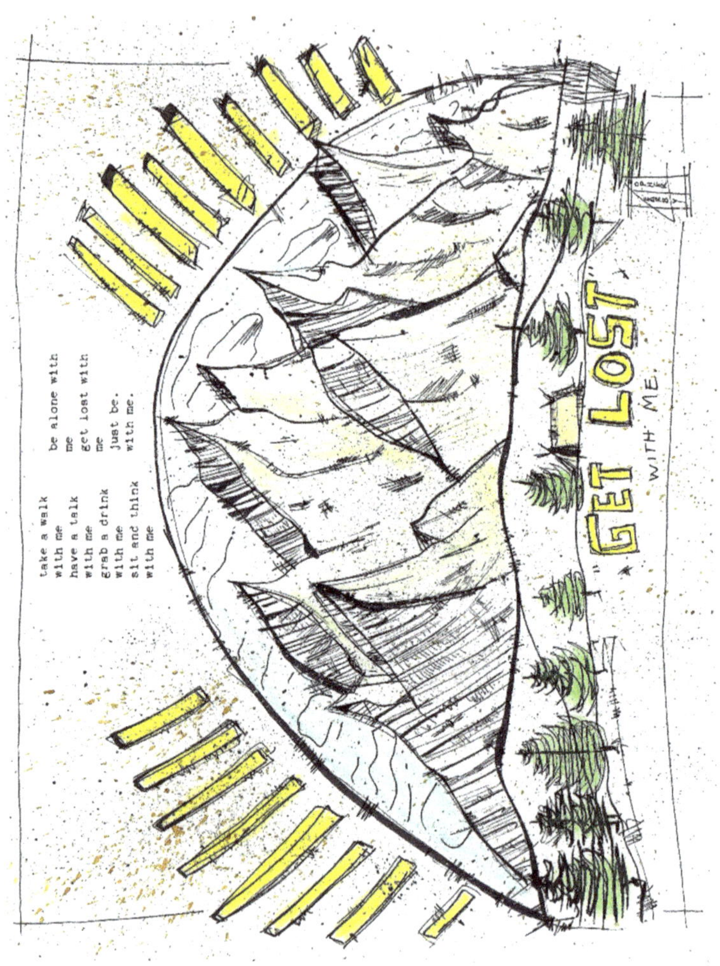
take a walk
with me
have a talk
with me
grab a drink
with me
sit and think
with me
be alone with
me
get lost with
me
just be.
with me.
"GET LOST"
WITH ME.

www.ingramcontent.com/pod-product-compliance
Ingram Content Group UK Ltd.
Pitfield, Milton Keynes, MK11 3LW, UK
UKHW062309290726
14090UKWH00018B/970